# How to Use Action Research in the Self-Renewing School

Emily F. Calhoun

Association for Supervision and Curriculum Development
Alexandria, Virginia

**About the Author**

Emily F. Calhoun is Director of the Phoenix Alliance in Saint Simons Island, Georgia. She has facilitated school-based and districtwide renewal programs and conducted extensive studies on the action research process. In her present position, Calhoun continues the work she began as teacher, curriculum consultant, county language arts coordinator, and coordinator of the University of Georgia League of Professional Schools. Address correspondence to the author at 624 Demere Way, Saint Simons Island, GA 31522.

**ASCD**™

Association for Supervision and Curriculum Development
1703 N. Beauregard St. • Alexandria, VA 22311-1714 USA
Telephone: 1-800-933-2723 or 703-578-9600 • Fax: 703-575-5400
Web site: http://www.ascd.org • E-mail: member@ascd.org

Ronald S. Brandt, *Executive Editor*
Nancy Modrak, *Managing Editor, Books*
Carolyn R. Pool, *Associate Editor*
Jennifer Beun, *Assistant Editor*
Gary Bloom, *Manager, Design and Production Services*
Stephanie A. Justen, *Print Production Coordinator*
Valerie Sprague, *Desktop Publisher*

ASCD Stock No.: 194030
ASCD member price: $6.95
Nonmember price: $8.95

**Library of Congress Cataloging-in-Publication Data**

Calhoun, Emily.
    How to use action research in the self-renewing school / Emily F. Calhoun.
        p.    cm.
    Includes bibliographical references.
    ISBN 0-87120-229-8 : $6.95
    1. Action research in education—United States.  2. School improvement programs—United States.    I. Title.
    LB1028.24.C25    1994
    370'.78—dc20                                                94-8999
                                                                CIP

01  00  99  98        5  4  3

# How to Use Action Research in the Self-Renewing School

# Preface

THIS BOOK IS ABOUT SCHOOLWIDE ACTION RESEARCH; IT REVIEWS THE *who, what, why, when, where,* and *how* of conducting schoolwide action research in the self-renewing school.

My primary purpose here is to help more school faculties have an opportunity to engage in schoolwide action research. My primary goals as a practitioner are to enhance the education of students and to develop healthier workplace norms for adults. Blending my purpose for communication with my primary goals, I offer this book to those who are seeking to make better choices in how we spend student and adult time and energy in our schools.

Throughout this book, I use the pronouns *I* and *we* and *you* in an attempt to diminish the distance between author and readers. I wish to convey the same sense of colleagueship that I experience when working with school faculties as they discover the potential of schoolwide action research in creating a healthier learning community. I also wish to remind you that I am sharing my experiences in schoolwide action research. Though I have studied the foundations of action research and its theoretical and research base, as well as school faculties engaging in this activity, many of my recommendations come from my experiences as a facilitator and student of the action research process.

I would like to extend special thanks to the sixty-one schools that compose the Georgia League of Professional Schools and the eleven Ames, Iowa, Community Schools whose faculties and school facilitator teams have allowed me the joy of learning and studying with them. I also thank both Carl Glickman and Bruce Joyce for their counsel and their willingness to help me reflect on and refine my ideas about school renewal through action research.

EMILY F. CALHOUN

# 1.
# Introducing Schoolwide Action Research

SCHOOLWIDE ACTION RESEARCH IS A FANCY WAY OF SAYING, "Let's study what's happening at our school, decide if we can make it a better place by changing what and how we teach and how we relate to students and the community; study the effects; and then begin again." It is a "rolling" (Huberman 1992) rather than a "lock step" model for changing the workplace.

The primary focus of this book is on studying what's happening to students, but we can also use action research to study and improve what's happening to adults in our learning community or to study the relationship of the school to the neighborhood. Our study can be large scale, using data from several years, such as the cumulative effects of schooling; something on a small scale, such as the immediate academic and social effects of the new social studies curriculum on students; or a combination of cumulative and immediate effects.

## The Action Research Cycle

In conducting schoolwide action research, we structure routines for continuous confrontation with data on the health of our school community. These routines are loosely guided by our movement through five phases of inquiry: faculty members select an area or problem of collective interest; they collect, organize, and interpret on-site data related to this area of interest; and they take action based

1

on this information (Calhoun 1991, Glickman 1990). These phases inherently overlap, and action researchers constantly retrace their steps and revise earlier phases before (or while) going forward again. This collective inquiry into our work (teaching) and its effects on students (learning and development) is a cyclic process and can serve as formative evaluation of initiatives we undertake as a school community. Figure 1.1 shows the five phases of the action research cycle.

To support major initiatives and to benefit from the collective wisdom of other educators and institutions, schoolwide action research includes a study of the available professional literature. We combine the information from

**Figure 1.1**
**The Action Research Cycle**

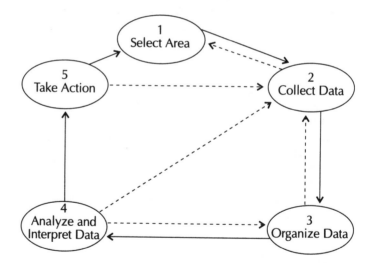

*Note:* The solid bold lines indicate the primary direction of the action research cycle from Phase 1, Selecting an Area of Focus for Study, to Phase 5, Taking Action.

The dotted lines indicate common moves (rolling back and then forward again) that occur as faculty members seek to refine or clarify information and identify the effects of actions being taken.

this study with the results of on-site data to determine what actions we will take to achieve commonly valued goals. Figure 1.2 shows a funnel with on-site data from our school and with data from other schools, districts, or the literature being "poured" into the collective decision-making process of our faculty.

Of course, schoolwide action research is no panacea. It offers no magic potion to give us automatic, painless school improvement. Yet the unknown potential of school renewal may well come to us through the collective study and search for improvement that occurs as we mount our own research and development efforts within each school. Serious study and collective action based on the results of our study make us intolerant of the status quo that allows the loss of a million students a year, with disenfranchisement from the opportunities our society offers beginning as early as kindergarten.

**Figure 1.2**
**Action Research Funnel:**
**Mixing Internal and External Information**

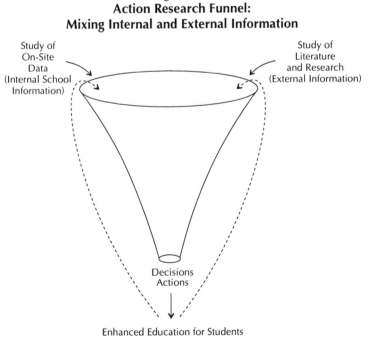

Study of
On-Site
Data
(Internal School
Information)

Study of
Literature
and Research
(External Information)

Decisions
Actions

Enhanced Education for Students

Healthier Workplace Norms for Adults

Although the interest of the public and of our local, state, and national governments has helped build a more favorable climate for initiating productive changes, the process cannot be conducted by persons external to the school. The school is where renewal happens, and the process begins with ourselves. We are the ones to reform first. Our professional role is not to "fix society." We cannot change the home environment of many of our children; nor can we immediately improve the socioeconomic status of the families who depend on us to provide an education for their children. What we can do immediately is to make better choices about how we spend student and adult time and energy in our schools.

Thus, a simple but essential component of school renewal may be individual and collective self-renewal: an orientation to work that means we are willing to accept the discomfort and joy of never finishing our education, of never graduating from our study of teaching. We learn from Fullan and Pomfret (1977) that one of the greatest difficulties for schools engaging in curriculum change revolves around the necessary changes in role relationships. Whether you review the research reports of Miles, Huberman, Rosenholtz, Louis, or Lieberman or read the reflections of Sarason or Bennis, you will continually confront the difficulties of behavioral change for those responsible for "progress."

What I find in many of these descriptions and in my experiences is that many of us want *others* to change: students, colleagues, principals, district office personnel, parents, the world. In the early stages of understanding school renewal, we are far less clear that we are actually asking ourselves to change. Many of us wish to fix, speed up, or remove others who appear to us to impede progress, specifically certain colleagues, our principal, someone from the district office, and certain members of our board of education. A gutsy article by Muncey and McQuillan (1993) reminds us that even when school faculties have an articulated consensus for schoolwide change, it may only happen for a few students and teachers, as it often has in the past.

Our mission of school improvement is a difficult one (this may be the understatement of the decade). Yet, we have reams and disks filled with information that we can use to help us move forward—information that can be combined with our individual and collective expertise and with the on-site data about life in our schools. We have information about how school faculties experience change, about concerns of teachers as they experience innovation, and about the effects of innovations on student learning. Documents that witness the lives and reflections of our colleagues across the years are there for our study and reflection. We can use these professional "gifts of experience" to inform our decisions and actions as we create healthier workplaces for ourselves and our students.

## School Improvement Scenarios

To see what a difference action research makes, let's look at two schools involved in school improvement efforts—one with and one without schoolwide action research (Calhoun 1992).

### Scenario for School 1

Thomas Elementary School joined the League of Professional Schools in 1990. During the spring, its leadership team and faculty developed an action plan with three main goals: to improve student self-esteem, to improve discipline, and to provide alternative strategies for instruction. Thomas faculty began to gather schoolwide baseline information about their students. As data were gathered and organized, characteristics began to emerge that identified Thomas as different from other elementary schools in the district: 42 percent of the students in grades 4–6 had been retained at least once (twice, for many); 30 percent of the students were either in resource or special needs classes; 51 percent of the students were from single-family homes; and 83 percent received free or reduced-price lunches. Study teams reviewed the professional literature, seeking information relevant to their collective goals. As the schoolwide data began to clarify the severity of the problems they and their students were facing, task forces and liaison groups involving all school personnel and parents worked to identify actions that would result in social and academic improvements for their students. Some of these actions were implemented immediately; others, within weeks; and others, such as all teachers' adding advanced cooperative learning strategies to their repertoire, took several years to implement fully. Thomas Elementary School is engaging in schoolwide action research.

### Scenario for School 2

Zeus High School also started its school improvement efforts in the spring of 1990. It also had liaison groups, task forces, and a leadership team, a majority of whose members were teachers. Its action plan focused on developing a process plan for school improvement efforts. Small-group meetings and total faculty meetings and memorandums abounded throughout the year. Zeus High School's 1991–92 action plan focused on developing a three- to five-year comprehensive school improvement plan; no focus on instruction evolved, and no schoolwide data on students have been collected. Although faculty members have been active, and the goal of their action plan has been reached, their picture of student life at Zeus has not been clarified. Zeus High School is not engaging in action research for the educational enhancement of its learning community.

### Comparison of School 1 and School 2

The Thomas school succeeded in capturing the collective energy of the action research process and increased its efficacy as an educational institution. Its students became more engaged in education, and its faculty became more professional as they became more successful. This school increased its capability to bring about desirable changes. Zeus was mired in self-concern. On the surface, it, too, was engaged in action research. But the social dynamic of its workplace, while consuming as many hours in planning, did not succeed in breaking away from the boundaries of its cultural norms, as did the process of School 1. For a variety of expressed reasons, ranging from "We need more time to plan" to "Sharing results publicly on how students are doing will cause unhealthy competition among us as teachers," instruction and its effects remained behind closed doors and not a matter for the professional collective.

Is your school or district more like School 1 or School 2? All of us—individuals and organizations alike—would rate somewhere between poor and excellent in our use of information to enhance our problem-solving capability. Action research can help us build this capability, but our initial efforts as we learn the process may feel messy because implementing action research for school improvement involves restructuring relationships, acquiring new skills, and learning to be active organizational problem-solvers.

My thesis on how to develop the school as a center of inquiry (Schaefer 1967) is simple, yet its implementation requires a will beyond what is usually demanded of us. Essentially, school renewal—and the action research needed to guide school renewal—is propelled by will. The NIKE™ ad, "JUST DO IT!" seems to capture the essence that distinguishes the schools that achieve their instructional goals from those that become mired in an endless process of planning or endure long hours of labor without any effects on students' social or academic achievement.

## Types of Action Research

We are currently seeing many articles, many conferences, and a great deal of new interest in action research. Like nongraded school programs, integrated language arts programs, and interrelated curriculum units, action research was a popular initiative years ago. In the 1940s and '50s, drawing largely on the work of Kurt Lewin and his colleagues and their development of a collective problem-solving cycle for improving life in organizations (Lewin 1947, 1948; Corey 1953), educators heralded action research as a process for supporting what we might call today "building community while attaining organizational goals."

The term *action research*, then as now, captures the notion of disciplined inquiry (thus, "research") in the context of focused efforts to improve the quality of the organization and its performance (thus, "action").

Recognized then as a powerful tool for simultaneously improving practice and the health of the organization, such is its appeal today. For teachers, principals, and district office personnel, action research promises progress in professionalization. By centering action on the careful collection of data to diagnose problems, a disciplined search for alternative solutions, an agreement to act, and the conscientious monitoring of whether and how much the solution worked—with a recycling of the process, either attacking the problem again or focusing on another one—we live the problem-solving process for ourselves and model it for our students. The potential is the development of a professional ethos in which members of the organization continually strive to improve their performance by learning to solve more and more problems (Corey 1953, Joyce 1991, Schaefer 1967, Sirotnik 1987).

As I have studied the literature about action research and related processes, I have found that the current movement is taking several forms that share two concepts from the earlier era: *the work centers on the practitioner*—this is research by educators, mostly teachers and administrators—and the practitioner-researchers use *disciplined inquiry*. However, I found three important differences among the current approaches to action research. One major difference is how many people are involved—whether the inquiry is conducted by individual teachers, by a small collaborative group, or by the entire school faculty. Other differences arise from variations in the degree of concern for achieving equity for students, for improving the organization as a problem-solving unit, and for developing collegial relations among teachers. These contrasts among the approaches are as important as the elements they share. Because the several types are all referred to by the same term, *action research*, we need to clarify their distinctive features because they reflect quite different conceptions of the workplace and quite different long-term objectives.

Selecting one type over another—individual teacher research, collaborative action research, or schoolwide action research—has important implications for the school renewal process that will take place. However, the use of one type of action research in any given setting does not mean that other types might not be used in the same setting. Each type has its virtues and its different purposes and results (Calhoun 1993). *The key to selection is what purpose the participants wish their inquiry to serve.*

### The Individual Teacher as Researcher

The purpose of individual teacher research is usually focused on changes in a single classroom. Teachers may notice something they wish to change or explore in terms of classroom climate, management, instructional strategies or materials, or students' cognitive or social behavior. Essentially, the teacher defines an area of interest—generally a problem to be solved—and seeks solutions to the problem, for example: improving student writing through use of the laptop computer (Marick 1990); determining if a particular teaching strategy improves race relations (Hopkins 1985); exploring the use of "Versatile" comprehension kits on the reading comprehension skills of at-risk, 3rd grade students; and using action research to develop a unit of instruction for students (Dicker 1990).

The primary audience for the results of individually conducted teacher research is, of course, the teacher conducting the research. If students have participated directly in the investigation, helping to generate and explore alternatives and determine effects, then they, too, form part of the primary audience. Several teachers within the same school may be conducting action research on a similar problem; they may or may not discuss their experiences or share the results of their exploration. The amount of sharing depends on the collegiality of the individuals. Where such sharing occurs, collegiality at the school may be enhanced (see, e.g., Myers 1985; Oja and Smulyan 1989; Rogers, Haven-O'Donnell, Hebdon, and Ferrell 1990; Strickland 1988).

### Collaborative Action Research

Depending on the number of teachers involved, the purpose of collaborative action research could be focused on problems and changes in a single classroom or on several classrooms within a school or district or across schools and districts. The size of the action research team may be as few as two people, or it may include several teachers and administrators working with one or more staff members from a university or other external agency. These collaborative action researchers might tackle a problem they share across their classrooms; they might focus on only one classroom; or they might tackle a districtwide problem. They follow the same investigative/reflective cycle as the individual teacher-researcher follows.

Here are some examples of collaborative action research conducted by two or more people: exploring changes in student achievement and attitudes through implementing a whole-language environment in three classrooms; studying the effects of a cooperative learning strategy, Teams-Games-Tournaments, on students' social and academic behaviors in two middle school classrooms; studying student responses to the new science units developed by the curriculum committee (a pilot study involving five classrooms in five schools); and improving students' skills in mathematical problem solving through the use of writing (one classroom and one teacher, one paraprofessional, one district office administrator, and one university professor participating in the study).

Articles and descriptions of collaborative action research often refer to joint work engaged in by teachers or administrators working with university personnel, intermediate service agency personnel, or facilitators of an educational consortium (see, e.g., Allen, Combs, Hendricks, Nash, and Wilson 1988; Holly 1991; Oja and Smulyan 1989; Sagor 1991; Whitford, Schlecty, and Shelor 1987). Although this joint work between school practitioners and research team participants from other organizations is collaborative, and members from both sets exploit the advantages of the union, teachers particularly benefit from the almost tutorial or coaching role these external personnel play. By working with faculty members and modeling the action research process, these external professionals help school personnel develop greater skill in using the tools of social science inquiry.

The primary audience for results from collaborative action research is the members of the research team. Depending on their degree of involvement in formulating and shaping the investigation, students and parents may form part of the primary audience. If these collaborative efforts are officially or fiscally sponsored by the school administration, the district office, or the university, then they, too, form part of the primary audience.

## Schoolwide Action Research

The purpose of schoolwide action research is school improvement, in three senses. One is the improvement of the organization as a problem-solving entity. Through repeated cycles of research, the faculty as a collegial group should become better and better able to work together to identify problems and solve them.

The second meaning refers to an improvement in equity for students. For example, if the faculty studies the writing process to offer better instructional opportunities for students, the intent is that *all students benefit*, not just those taught by a few faculty members.

The third implication of schoolwide action research is the breadth and content of the inquiries themselves. If the faculty decides to study the writing process, the teachers intend the quality of writing to improve *throughout the school*. And in an area of common concern or interest, every classroom and every teacher are involved in collective study and regular assessment of effects on students. As they strive for schoolwide growth, faculty members may involve students and parents, and even the general community, in data collection and interpretation and in the selection of options for action.

Of course, schoolwide action research is also collaborative, but it is different from what is termed *collaborative action research* in that everyone in the school is involved in the inquiry.

Here are some examples of schoolwide action research: explore and improve student performance in mathematics; improve student self-esteem and student achievement across all subject areas; improve the social skills of students through implementing cooperative learning across the curriculum; and increase student use of technology to accomplish communication tasks (especially computer use for writing, graphics display, and data bases).

Formal schoolwide inquiry is often initiated in a school because of its affiliation with a league or consortium that promotes action research as a major school improvement strategy—such as the Center for Leadership in School Reform in Kentucky or the League of Professional Schools in Georgia. Some school leadership teams and district administrators who have read about action research, attended awareness sessions about it, or discussed it with peers who are using it have worked to apply it in their home settings.

The audience for the results of schoolwide action research includes all primary participants. Thus the smallest audience possible is the total school faculty. School faculty members, as a group, may decide to expand this audience to include students, parents, the general community, and the school board.

\*    \*    \*

The schoolwide, collective action variation may be the most complex type of action research to implement, because it *asks for participation in achieving schoolwide goals from all members of the organization we call school.* Collecting schoolwide data on an instructional initiative—such as improving student achievement in language arts, mathematics, or science—requires collegial trust and mental and physical collaboration. Marshalling the efforts of all, both takes and provides energy; supporting each other through the anxieties of public sharing of the immediate effects of actions on students in each classroom requires initial patience and understanding of self and others. Schoolwide action research may feel messy and uneven, and conflict may arise during the first few cycles—all of which is to be expected when a diverse community is learning to apply a complex process. However, the very complexity generates important side effects: chiefly, that all participants have to learn a lot about building colleagueship, about managing the group process, and about aspects of curriculum and instruction that they might not have reflected on had they worked alone.

As you may have noticed, the student learning goals of the inquiry may be the same in individual, collaborative, and schoolwide action research. The major differentiators in this typology of action research are the number of adults directly involved in the inquiry and the number of students directly affected through the modeling of the process and the actions taken as a result of and as part of the inquiry. For schoolwide renewal, the more people we involve directly, the more likely we are to enhance the education of all students and of ourselves as members of a rich and diverse community.

Many teachers and administrators have engaged in productive curricular and instructional improvement through each type of action research. In many cases, collaborative relationships have increased among school personnel and members of central district offices, intermediate agencies, and universities and their personnel. When schoolwide action research has been implemented, the problem-solving capabilities of schools and even districts have increased. Moreover, the use of one type of research does not exclude another. Individual and collaborative research may nest comfortably and productively within schoolwide action research. The Appendix of this book contains examples of policies and data-collection forms that other schools have found useful (Items 1–5). In addition, Item 6 contains reflections on commonly asked questions about action research— questions you might encounter as you begin the process.

Before reading the next chapter, think about your content area background and your experiences in schools and with other organizations or groups. What does the schoolwide action research process remind you of? For me, it's like a group problem-solving strategy as in the old Carkhuff (1973) materials, like a giant group investigation, like the scientific method, like empirical problem-solving in mathematics, like a group information-processing technique, like the research process I learned in social studies. What it's not like is "pure" research or schoolwide experimental research. Though individual teachers or collaborative groups may design experimental studies to investigate different aspects of their collective initiative, *schoolwide action research is primarily a process of collecting data about an ongoing system (our school) with the purpose of improving practice (teaching and learning).*

13

# 2
# Establishing a Conceptual Framework

TOO OFTEN IN EDUCATION, WE IGNORE THE THEORETICAL BASIS AND history supporting the ideas and innovations we adopt. We invest our energy and resources in popular innovations without investigating their history. For teachers and administrators just thinking about or beginning action research—and for other students like myself—this chapter provides a glimpse into the origins of action research for organizational improvement and how action research relates to school renewal.

Your faculty or district can engage in action research for schoolwide change if you establish a common goal, regularly collect and share information about that goal, and make collective decisions or take action as indicated. It's as simple as that.

Or it would be simple, if we were accustomed to doing it. The acts of collecting information, formulating goals, selecting actions, implementing them, and collecting information about their effects are not technically difficult. However, these actions require faculties to develop quite different patterns of interaction than have been normative. We need a compass to guide us through the new patterns and to help us avoid drifting back into the ones that have kept so many schools from developing collective energy.

Thus, I find it useful to have a conceptual framework to guide my facilitation of action research. It helps me maintain a reasonable balance of confidence and uncertainty. The conceptual framework that guides my practice is a formulation of Lewin's action research and group dynamics; of Dewey's problem-solving approach to education; of Thelen's integrated spheres of knowledge, inquiry, and dynamics; and Schaefer's inquiry, not activity, as a fulcrum for growth and understanding.

Each of these conceptual mentors recognized that social organizations tend to settle into practices and ways of interaction that can become self-perpetuating. A normative structure forms that becomes self-protecting. Unless a process for renewal develops, and the organization adapts continually, the passage of time will ensure incremental drift toward obsolescence. What seemed to work at one time will lose its potency. Problems that seemed small will fester and grow larger. Technological developments will fail to be incorporated into practice. Lewin, Dewey, Thelen, and Schaefer generated the means to create an inquiring, adapting organization better for its clients and its workers.

The following is an overview of where action research came from and why it should work.

## The Origins of Action Research

Over the years, the general ideas underlying action research have been applied to a wide range of purposes: from trying to make organizations more efficient, to generating more healthy social groups, to addressing major social problems such as reducing anti-Semitism and racial prejudice. In applications to education, action research addresses the problem of organizational effectiveness in service of the client (the school improvement application) while simultaneously addressing the need to create a more collegial and satisfying workplace and to reduce the isolation that has separated teachers from teachers and teachers from administrators and community members.

The origin of formal action research is usually attributed to Kurt Lewin (1947, 1948) and his students (e.g., Lippitt). Lewin's integration of action-taking into experimental social science research was published in 1946 in "Action Research and Minority Problems" and in 1947 in "Group Decisions and Social Change." Both articles define action research as a three-step spiral process of (1) planning, which involves "reconnaissance or fact-finding"; (2) taking actions; and (3) fact-finding about the results of the action (Lewin 1948).

Lewin stated:

> Planning starts usually with something like a general idea. For one reason or another it seems desirable to reach a certain objective. Exactly how to circumscribe this objective and how to reach it is frequently not too clear (p. 205).

Lewin's description of planning matches how most schools approach the development of their action plans. The faculty or leadership teams often have a general area of interest or concern in mind before initial data on students are collected. Thus, they reach intuitively toward general goals and means and gradually progress toward a plan specific enough to act on.

Lewin (1947) believed that social problems should be served by social inquiry. His action research approach that applied the methodology of social science to immediate, practical, major problems developed out of his work to improve intergroup relations within organizations and communities. Lewin challenged the compartmentalization of research from action and the separation of research personnel from active players. He advocated including practitioners from the arena under investigation in all phases of the research. He also challenged practitioners to use the tools of the social scientist to bring about change: "It seems to be crucial for the progress of social science that the practitioner understand that through social sciences and only through them can he gain the power necessary to do a good job" (Lewin 1948, p. 213).

Lewin and others who developed the action research concept emphasized collective rather than individualistic problem solving and study. Thus, action researchers study problems that grow out of the community, work within a group to determine actions to be taken, and evaluate the effect of these actions within the community setting. Lewin (1947) advocated group work as part of the action research process because of the power of group discussion and interaction in producing commitment and because of the support for changes in individual attitudes and behavior provided by group interaction. Chein, Cook, and Harding (1948) recommended practitioner involvement to build awareness of the need for the actions taken and greater personal investment in making the actions work.

Corey (1949, 1953) was one of the first to officially promote action research in the field of education. His definition of action research was the "process by which practitioners attempt to study their problems scientifically in order to guide, correct, and evaluate their decisions and actions" (1953, p. 6). His thesis was that school practitioners would make better decisions and implement more effective practices if they conducted research as part of their decision-making process and used the results of such research as a guide to selection or modification of their practice. The value of action research for Corey was "determined by the extent to which findings lead to improvement in the practices of the people engaged in the research" (p. 13). Through the involvement of teachers, administrators, and supervisors in studying their work (teaching) and in applying these findings to their school setting, changes would be more likely to occur.

Both Lewin and Corey worked with organizations to change the existing cultural norms. Their route to changing the standards of behavior from an individualistic, autonomous, and isolated mode to a collaborative and integrated mode was action research. Lewin described how the process of action, research, and training together can "transform . . . a multitude of unrelated individuals, frequently opposed in their outlook and their interests, into cooperative teams, not on the basis of sweetness but on the basis of readiness to face difficulties realistically, to apply honest fact-finding, and to work together to overcome them" (1946, p. 211).

Lewin's work in the 1940s with a variety of organizations—from single schools, to minority organizations, to labor and management representatives—has remarkable relevance for us today as we seek school renewal:

> Two basic facts emerged from these contacts: there exists a great amount of good-will, of readiness to face the problem squarely and really do something about it. . . . [Yet] these eager people feel themselves to be in the fog. They feel in the fog on three counts:

1. What is the present situation?
2. What are the dangers?
3. And most important of all, what shall we do? (1948, p. 201)

Lewin considered the lack of clarity about what ought to be done as one of the greatest obstacles to improvement of intergroup relations. He felt that one of the consequences of this confusion was the lack of standards by which to measure progress:

> In a field that lacks objective standards of achievement, no learning can take place. If we cannot judge whether an action has led forward or backward, if we have no criteria for evaluating the relation between effort and achievement, there is nothing to prevent us from making the wrong conclusions and to encourage the wrong work habits. Realistic fact-finding and evaluation is a prerequisite for any learning (Lewin 1948, p. 202).

Lewin also identified another "severe effect" of the inability to determine the relationship between efforts made and achievement. This failure to measure the effects of actions designed to lead to improved conditions within an organization deprives workers (teachers, administrators, general educators, and students) "of their legitimate desire for satisfaction on a realistic basis" (Lewin 1948, p. 202). Because descriptive fact-finding about educational innovations is not an integral operating behavior in most school cultures, satisfaction or dissatisfaction with achievement relative to an innovation remains personalized and is mainly a matter of individual "temperament." In my twenty-two years as an educator, I have found this to be true across most school districts, regardless of the simplicity or complexity of the innovation and regardless of its cost in money or time. From adopting a new handwriting program, to using manipulatives in K–8 mathematics instruction, to adopting a literature-based approach to language arts, to forming block schedules in the middle and high schools, to mainstreaming of students, and so on—we do very little formative, collective analysis of the effects of an innovation, accompanied by the use of that analysis to inform our decisions.

As long as the determination of success or failure of an innovation, even if it was originally selected by a team or a school council or the entire faculty, is left solely to us as individuals, collective action for school improvement or "site-based, collaborative school improvement" will be impossible. Professional satisfaction for members of a dynamic organization requires *collective acceptance of and responsibility for the continuous cycle of measuring progress and taking action.* Such a process builds individual and organizational efficacy: We can change things.

## Using Schoolwide Action Research for Renewal _____

> It is irresponsible for a school to mobilize, initiate, and act without any conscious way of determining whether such expenditure of time and energy is having a desirable effect.
> (Glickman 1993, pp. 54–55, *Renewing America's Schools*)

After almost thirty years in various stages of burial, action research for school improvement is once again receiving national attention. Today, Glickman (1990, 1993) is the major scholar supporting the use of schoolwide action research for school renewal. Glickman (1993) describes a framework of democratic governance, educational focus, and action research as integral dimensions of renewing education. Within this framework, the principles that guide shared decision making within the organization are expressed in a school "charter," the focus on teaching and learning is expressed in a school "covenant," and the school faculty uses the "critical study process" of action research to assess the results of its current programs on commonly valued goals.

Through schoolwide action research, a school faculty can develop the school as a center of inquiry so that it is perpetually self-renewing. The formal collection of data, followed by group analysis and interpretation, can move our school community forward in the path it has elected to follow. This regular confrontation with data as a progress marker can function as "choice points" for our organization, as both "noticing choice" and "doing choice." Paraphrasing Weick (1969, pp. 59–60) on the role of choice in the organizing process, the school community can ask itself: "Knowing what we know now, should we *notice* something we did not notice before and ignore something we noticed before?" and "Knowing what we know now, should we act differently?" From baseline data to regular checks on

19

progress, we intentionally confront ourselves with a series of choice points for unfreezing action and changing the experience of schooling. In the self-renewing school, this collective inquiry and study may evolve into something that looks quite different from its debut into the culture of the school, but it never ends. The faculty continues the cycle of "noticing" and "acting" as they create even more powerful and healthy learning communities.

Figure 2.1 shows four definitions of action research for organizational improvement. As you review these definitions, think about their common elements.

---

**Figure 2.1**

**Definitions of Action Research
for Organizational Improvement**

Action research is a three-step spiral process of (1) planning which involves reconnaissance or fact-finding; (2) taking actions; and (3) fact-finding about the results of the action.

(Kurt Lewin 1947)

Action research is a process by which practitioners attempt to study their problems scientifically in order to guide, correct, and evaluate their decisions and actions.

(Stephen Corey 1953)

Thus action research in education is study conducted by colleagues in a school setting of the results of their activities to improve instruction.

(Carl Glickman 1990)

Action research is a fancy way of saying, "Let's study what's happening at our school and decide how to make it a better place."

(Emily Calhoun, this work)

---

How can these common elements (problems identified by persons within the organization, the inquiry approach to solving these problems, and a high degree of practitioner involvement and interaction) support school renewal? When you begin to visualize how these elements would operate in your school, you have established a rough conceptual framework to guide your implementation of schoolwide action research.

As you can tell, action research or data used to guide the actions of members of an organization is conceptually simple; it sounds, looks, and feels much like slightly formalized problem solving, which it is. The regular application of this approach as a normal way of doing business, in making the school a center of inquiry, however, is difficult to accomplish (Sirotnik 1987). Whether in schools (Goodlad 1984) or in business and industry (Lippitt, Langseth, and Mossop 1985), answers to the question "What has been accomplished through the changes implemented by the organization?" are not readily available to most stakeholders.

Lippitt and coworkers (1985) cite two surveys that address the lack of evaluation in planned organizational change in business and industry. First, of 160 published reports of change interventions examined by Porras and Berg, only 20 included evaluation components to assess organizational or work-group changes. It is interesting to examine the reasons. Second, in a survey of 76 consultants and clients, Bidwell and Lippitt found four major factors cited as obstacles to the evaluation of organizational changes: lack of time, lack of criteria or a frame of reference, inability to develop measurable objectives, and lack of money. What is of interest to us is that these four factors include the same ones identified by Lewin (1948) and those identified by members of the Georgia League of Professional Schools (Calhoun 1991, 1992) in relation to their assessment of progress on their initiatives, especially time, criteria, and measurable objectives.

However, I believe we learn how to assess our progress on a common goal simply by doing it. We learn how to conduct schoolwide action research by conducting it. As school teams struggle to determine how they will measure their school improvement goals, both the goals and the routes or actions to take in achieving them should become more clear. Effective schools demonstrate improved achievement over time; they regularly collect and use data to assess student performance (Glickman 1990, p. 253). We know that the action research process of identifying problem areas and ideas worth pursuing, gathering relevant data, discussing these data, formulating solutions, determining actions, and assessing the effects of these actions is a capacity currently "lacking in most schools" (Goodlad 1984, p. 276). This knowledge should not inhibit our quest for school renewal. Fortunately, schools in the United States exist in a national culture that has long revered a pragmatic, problem-solving approach. Because of the support for this approach to change in our macro-system, the capacity for action research for school improvement could be rapidly developed within our schools.

\* \* \*

Action research for school renewal unites work from Dewey, Lewin, and Schaefer. Their combined wisdom and experience provide us with powerful pathways to educational enhancement. Drawing heavily from Dewey's pragmatic, problem-solving, experiential approach to education; from Lewin's understanding of how people function within their environment and use of this understanding to promote collective action for social change; and from Schaefer's concept of the school as the center of inquiry, we can confidently seek paths of actualization for our students, for ourselves, and for the organizations within which we live. The tools of the scientific method, combined with social learning theory and group dynamics, provide a firmly constructed framework for us to explore and expand as part of the current wave of restructuring and reform.

We can also draw on a new generation of research on the social system of the school and on recent action research to help us smooth out the process and make it more effective at our school sites (see Bibliography for works by Calhoun, David and Peterson, Glickman and Allen, Holly, Huberman, Joyce and Calhoun, Rosenholtz, and Louis and Miles).

Moreover, we should not underestimate the value of encouraging all actors in the school community (parents, students, teachers, administrators, and central office) to be engaged in information seeking and empirical problem solving aimed at making their world—from student life at the classroom table, to classroom instruction, to the school schedule—a healthier place, socially, intellectually, and physically. Added to the rich diversity of participants engaging in this collective inquiry is the value of our modeling lifelong learning and problem solving in the professional environment in which we have chosen to live. This modeling supports and enriches our personal, professional growth (Dewey 1904; Gardner 1963, 1987; Houle 1980; Schön 1987) and provides continuous demonstrations of these critical life processes for our students. Or, simply stated, actions speak louder than words, and what we do carries more weight than what we say. What are the real "basics" we as educators wish to convey? As Schaefer (1967) stated in his grand essay:

> How to induce more children to grapple zestfully with academic issues may elude our most determined efforts. But I strongly suspect that observing adults honestly wrestling with intellectual problems might win more youngsters to the life of the mind than any other experience the schools could devise (p. 77).

As you engage in this process of collective inquiry within your school, you will personalize your own path or conceptual framework for conducting schoolwide action research. Such a framework has much to do with understanding where you are going and how to get there successfully.

# 3
# Implementing Schoolwide Action Research

THE MAJOR PORTION OF MY ADVICE ON IMPLEMENTING SCHOOLWIDE action research involves how to establish the conditions and structures that support the effort. The approach I recommend goes back to the NIKE ad: "Just Do It!" I find too many faculties getting stuck in the readiness and planning stages, thus prohibiting their development of any sense of collective efficacy—and I do not want my suggestions to reinforce that tendency. However, the following six tangible conditions and three intangible beliefs can support the initiation and maintenance of schoolwide action research. And the careful tending of the implementation by members of all role groups can lead to immediate student benefits and to a healthier workplace for all members of the organization.

As you read this chapter, ask yourself, "Where is my school as an organization in relation to this condition?" Then ask yourself, "How do I feel personally about this condition?" and "How would my worklife change if this condition were operating fully in my school?"

## Tangible Conditions That Need to Be Established_____

The following six *recommendations* support the successful implementation of schoolwide action research; *they are not a rigid list of prerequisites.*

## 1. A Faculty That Seeks a Better Education for Its Students

If you are part of a faculty that has a majority of teachers working together for increased student effects, you are already off to a great beginning. Just introduce the concept of schoolwide action research. If the majority of the faculty is receptive to the process, get going on a common goal or on collecting baseline data and study the action research process as you engage in it. Or, getting started could involve more study and discussion, as follows.

Someone at your school is exposed to the idea of school renewal through schoolwide action research. This someone could be you—a teacher, administrator, media specialist, lead teacher, whatever your role. This exposure could occur through reading an article in a journal or book, through a session you attended at a conference, through discussions with colleagues in a school or a district engaging in action research. In other words, someone brings the idea to the chief administrator and teachers in your building.

If your school has a leadership team in place and its members are receptive to the idea of collective study and action, they may pursue clarification of the action research process. These members may collect additional articles; contact other schools using schoolwide action research and ask their leadership teams for information; and ask the central office, local intermediate service agency, or local university personnel for information. As these group members study the information and think about using action research in their school, they may decide at this point to share the best articles or resources they have found with all their colleagues and to introduce the idea at a faculty meeting. The purpose of presenting the idea and engaging in discussion and questions is increasing *awareness,* not necessarily making a decision to initiate schoolwide action research.

The majority of the faculty may decide immediately, "Yes, let's try this." Or they may say, "It sounds interesting, but let's find out more." Then you begin a more formal review of the resources collected. After a few weeks of study and discussion by faculty members, you may want to bring in someone who is using action research to bring about improved benefits for students in a nearby school, preferably a teacher and an administrator, or someone who has technical expertise in conducting schoolwide action research. If you cannot afford to bring someone in or there are no schools nearby, you may be able to get a school team to make a videotape presentation for you—a sort of talking-heads tape.

I find that school faculties may be ready for a decision on whether to use schoolwide action research anywhere from a few days to a couple of months after the idea is introduced. And this is a tricky time, even when the staff is receptive. You do not want the introductory activities to take too long, but you do want participants to understand what they are committing themselves to.

A school faculty composed of members who are satisfied with the status quo of education offered their students and with the effects of this education on their students' lives would not be receptive to schoolwide action research. And we know that a good autocratic principal can, with faculty support, bring about school changes, such as modifications in Chapter 1 programs, adoptions of new basals, application of the principles of effective schools, and so on; and the same is true of a small powerful group of teachers within the school (David and Peterson 1984; Louis and Miles 1990). However, the process of school renewal through schoolwide action research is so demanding that selling it to or imposing it on an unwilling faculty would probably be nonproductive. If only a small group of teachers is interested in working and studying together, then collaborative—not schoolwide—action research may be the best option.

## 2. A Public Agreement About How Collective Decisions Are Made

If your school has established a shared-decision-making process between building administrators and teachers, you are ahead of the game. I do not know whether you can use schoolwide action research if administrators and teachers do not share decisions concerning schoolwide instruction and curriculum—though it is probably possible in schools where administrators are advised by their teachers.

To establish a shared governance process in your school, the faculty may use our national governmental structures as a model:

- elect representative members to serve on a school facilitation team or school leadership team;
- specify the areas in which teachers and administrators will be equally responsible for decisions (one person, one vote on the facilitation team); and
- develop a charter that describes, in a page or two, how schoolwide decisions are made.

Look at Item 1 in the Appendix for an example of a charter developed by Thunderbolt Elementary School teachers and administrators to guide their collective decision-making process. For a full description of how to establish shared decision making in schools, read Glickman's (1993) *Renewing America's Schools*.

### 3. A Facilitation Team Willing to Lead the Action Research Process

Whether or not your faculty establishes a formal process for shared decision making, your school will need a facilitation team to support schoolwide action research. The members of this team may be representatives elected by the faculty or they may be volunteers who are willing to lead the action research process. These members serve the larger learning community as schoolwide facilitators. If your school already has such a team, great; if not, form one.

The team needs to include teachers and administrators. The chief school administrator serves on the team by virtue of her position of responsibility and leadership. The criteria for electing or selecting the other members of the facilitation team are very simple: people who are committed to enhancing the education of all members of their school organization, whether those members are 6 years old or 66 years old; people who are willing to share the leadership responsibility of actively tending the collective goals of the faculty; and people who are willing to study the process of schoolwide action research.

Members of the facilitation team will need to meet regularly, sometimes as frequently as once a week at the beginning of the action research process. The problem of providing meeting time for team members has been addressed by most schools. Here are some of their solutions:

- having paraprofessionals cover team members' classes the last hour of the day once a week;
- paying team members a token stipend for the year, then team members establish their meeting times;
- providing substitutes for one-half day once every four weeks;
- providing one "released" period or an hour of released time every day for the chair of the facilitation team or the person who is primarily responsible for organizing the data and organizing information for sharing with the faculty;
- meeting after school; and
- various combinations of these suggestions.

Once the facilitation team has been established, its members may want to conduct an informal organizational diagnosis of individual staff members' perceptions of current group work occurring in the school and a diagnosis of members' perceptions of how the staff works together as a learning community. Simple worksheets with a few questions can provide the team with an overview of the context for collective action in the school. Figure 3.1 shows some sample worksheets.

First, facilitation team members need to organize and study the responses to these questions. The task is to identify any patterns across responses and to identify any major or minor problems that need to be addressed. Then the team should share this information with all faculty members for their collective reflection and clarification.

Second, this information will be used to assist the team in their facilitation of the action research process and in developing the schoolwide plan to guide this process. As team members organize these responses and turn them into an information base, they generally identify many other uses. For example, when the sheer number of committees operating within the school community is displayed for faculty review, faculty members are often amazed—and they immediately abolish or combine some of them.

---

**Figure 3.1**

**Sample Worksheets**

**Learning Community Worksheet**

1. Describe how our staff works together.

2. Describe how our staff works with students, parents, and the community in making decisions.

3. Describe how our staff works with district office personnel in making decisions.

4. What needs tending to help our school move forward as a learning community?

**Organizational Diagnosis Worksheet**

1. What committees or groups are functioning in our school?

2. What are their purposes? How do they operate?

3. Do you have any recommendations to make about these committees or groups?

---

Another early task of the facilitation team is the *formulation of an action plan and timeline.* At first this may be an open plan that identifies major activities, persons involved, and dates. As soon as a collective goal has been identified by the faculty, the plan needs to become more specific in terms of data to be collected, research articles and reflective pieces from the professional literature to study, times to analyze and discuss the data as a faculty, and times to discuss the possibilities for collective action. If your school has a small faculty, you may develop the action plan as a total-group activity. If your school has a large faculty, the facilitation team may develop a tentative action plan and submit it to the faculty for review and suggestions. Providing members of the faculty with an opportunity to assist in the planning of their inquiry builds support for collective action and builds responsibility for its accomplishment. Providing everyone with a copy of the "completed" but malleable action plan and timeline is symbolic and pragmatic: it serves as a checklist for progress through the inquiry; it serves as a record of the experience for the faculty; and it publishes the major activities and commitments of the faculty.

A facilitation team is essential to the initiation of schoolwide action research. The major operational tasks of its members are to keep things moving and focused on collective goals and on the sharing and use of on-site data to inform the decision-making process. These facilitators help their colleagues *establish routines for working together, for making collective decisions, and for taking collective action as a united force.*

### 4. Study Groups or Liaison Groups That Meet Regularly

If you already have study groups operating in your school, great. If not, you will need them to support the action research process. They are critical for setting yourself up for successful implementation. They function as small learning communities within the larger school community.

These small collaborative groups whose members meet regularly seem to be necessary to support any large-scale implementation. We have known this for years (Crandall, Loucks, Huberman, and Miles 1982), and yet we generally fail to use them. They are needed to provide technical support, to provide social support, to expand our conceptual understanding through discussion, and to provide a forum for regular sharing of the effects of our instruction. They support us as we engage in new learning and as we take risks and try things not in our present repertoire. When functioning well, they operate much like good cooperative learning groups.

*The lack of time and the nature of the content of the study group sessions are frequent reasons given for our failure to establish these supportive learning environments.*

*Let's Take Time First.* I have no magic wand for this. And until we go to a full calendar year of employment in public schools with professional development time built in, we are stuck with re-creating how we use our current schoolday. Here are some examples of how school faculties have handled the problem of time for study group meetings:

• developing the school schedule for the year so that teachers on a study team have a common planning period;

• developing the school schedule for the year so that teachers on a study team have their students attending physical education, art, or music at the same time;

• using every other faculty meeting for study groups, in a school that had one faculty meeting each week;

• changing the requirement that teachers remain an extra 30 minutes after students have left to 15 minutes on four schooldays and meeting for an hour one afternoon a week;

• adding 15 minutes to each of four schooldays, releasing students an hour early on Wednesdays, and meeting for 2 hours;

• having paraprofessionals cover the classes of one study group team for 2 hours, with a set schedule that provides a meeting time for each study group every two weeks;

• meeting 1 hour before school once a week; and

• building the meeting times into the district's staff development program for the school.

Of course, many school faculties opt to simply meet for an hour every week, or every other week, after school. The frequency of these meetings is important. They need to be held often enough so that the focus of energy and study by each group is a live current in the school and so that staff members are discussing results, actions, student responses, and information from the professional literature. In other words, we use these meetings to keep the initiative alive as a mini-mission and to support individual professional development.

***Establishing Guidelines for Study Group Meetings.*** What happens when the study groups meet? During study group time, faculty members share and discuss the on-site data they have been collecting, build lessons based on the results of these data, discuss articles they have read or videotapes they have viewed, discuss the actions they are taking to support their common initiative and the implementation of these actions, share information from the school facilitation team, and determine what information or concerns need to be passed on to the facilitation team for discussion beyond the study group. These processes and tasks form the content of study group meetings.

I have a few structural recommendations on the formation of these groups:

1. Keep them small, four to six people each.
2. Make them cross-grade-level and cross-departmental.
3. Allow faculty members to form their own teams.
4. Have agendas or logs sent to the facilitation team after each meeting.
5. Schedule them weekly or biweekly.

First, the groups should be small because they are work groups, not forums for presentations. We use them to increase the amount of discussion about our initiative and to facilitate observations and peer coaching among group members. We use them to plan lessons together around our common goal and to support the implementation of new instructional strategies. Second, we want them cross-grade- level to support schoolwide, not just grade-level, under- standing and pursuit of our common initiative. In terms of prevention, we want to avoid the formation of four, five, or eight little "grade-level schools-within-the-school" that "look after 2nd grade interests" or "the needs of the English department." We need this mixture in these small learning communities for its diversity of perspectives and the enrichment that follows.

Third, we favor self-formation of teams because most of us like to have a choice of working partners. We simply ask faculty members to include a range of grade levels, special areas, and departments in their group. We want the interactions among the group members to be such that it decreases the reluctance on the part of some faculty members to "take down the walls of their classrooms" and share the effects of their craft; in other words, we want a nurturing environment. If the faculty asks the facilitation team to form groups for them, then do so.

Fourth, we ask for agendas, which may be handwritten, so that the facilitation team has an indicator of the effectiveness of the study group time in supporting the schoolwide initiative. The teams can also use this information as they plan support activities for the faculty.

Finally, we schedule regular group meetings because we need them to keep us focused. We use these sessions to keep the learning and dialogue alive. They function like a cross between a good seminar and a task force action group (a bit like the old *Mission Impossible* team).

### 5. Awareness and Some Understanding of the Action Research Cycle

To get started with schoolwide action research, faculty members need to study the action research cycle (see Figure 1.1) and the activities that compose each phase of the cycle (see Item 2 in the Appendix). An example of how to introduce the concept of action research to a school faculty was provided earlier in this chapter. And Chapter 2 includes information about the rationale for schoolwide action research. In this section, I wish to share a reminder about the necessary knowledge base and the rationale.

For some of us, full understanding of the process may be attained only after we have completed several cycles successfully and seen some benefits from our labors. Huberman and Miles (1984) remind us that competence precedes commitment. It's difficult to believe in something or to be good at something if we have little or no experience or practice with it. However, a basic conceptual understanding of the action research process and why it is useful appears to be an essential part of helping school faculties sustain their efforts (Calhoun 1992). All members of the facilitation team will need to understand the action research cycle if they are to effectively support their colleagues in this complex learning task; and each faculty member needs to accept and project support and patience for each other and for the learning community as a whole. *We need to articulate the developmental nature of learning to use schoolwide action research.* Few of us learn complex tasks the first time we try them. Be patient and supportive with yourselves as you implement the process.

Here's the rationale for conducting action research: Action research has the potential to help in self-renewal and in school renewal for these reasons:

• It emphasizes individual interactions within a group setting to support changes in behavior.

• Its cycles of fact-finding feed decision making and revising and evaluating actions.

• It is useful for addressing large-scale social problems—and school improvement requires resocialization.

• It goes beyond acquisition of knowledge toward action steps within the context studied.

• It provides opportunities for all actors within the school community to be engaged in group investigation and active problem solving.

More simply stated, *we are more powerful working together as an educational force for our students than we are working individually.*

After the concept of schoolwide action research has been introduced to the faculty and a decision has been made to proceed, the facilitation team may wish to take a reading of faculty members' perceptions of factors in the school environment that will support the implementation of action research, as well as factors that will inhibit it (Figure 3.2 shows some sample questions).

I suggest that you conduct this survey as part of a faculty session instead of sending it out to staff members. Gathering this information from each faculty member serves several purposes, including: (1) The facilitation team is modeling the action research process; and (2) identifying patterns that are present provides the facilitation team with an organized perspective on factors they can build on to support schoolwide action research and on factors they need to modify, eliminate, or address as part of their facilitation.

---

**Figure 3.2**

**Survey on Realities of Action Research**

**Enhancing Factors**

What do we have happening in our school that increases development of teacher thought and collective action pertaining to schoolwide action research?

**Impeding Factors**

What do we have happening in our school that hinders development of teacher thought and collective action pertaining to schoolwide action research?

---

## 6. Technical Assistance

Again, I say, set yourselves up for success. Most school faculties need technical assistance—human support from someone outside the school—to help them move forward in schoolwide action research. Teacher and administrator "buy-in" to shared decision making for schoolwide actions and the selection of a common focus are essential beginnings—but people still need assistance with the difficult task of learning action research and the stressful changes in the social interaction and norms.

The school facilitation team or the chief school administrator usually needs to find an objective and knowledgeable "outsider" who can provide support for at least the first year. This person may be from the district office, from another school that has used action research successfully (they have achieved measurable benefits for students), or from an intermediate service agency. Look for someone who understands school change and who knows how to collect multiple data sources—both perceptual and behavioral, using both quantitative and qualitative methods. This person should know how to organize these data for study by the faculty and how to help the facilitation team plan the study of on-site data by all members of the faculty. Optimally, this assistant "teaches and coaches" the team in methods of data collection and analysis while providing technical support.

# Intangible Beliefs That Support Schoolwide Action Research

We can structure five of the six tangible conditions into our worklife; in fact, we can build them in as we begin the action research process. But the intangible beliefs that support initiation and sustain implementation are not so readily promoted. A belief in collective problem solving, a belief in the value of information to inform decisions, and a belief in the developmental nature of implementation need to permeate the culture of a faculty that engages in cooperative inquiry. Facilitation team members tend these beliefs—which may be reflected initially in the behaviors of as few as two people in the school, but eventually need to be reflected in the behaviors of most staff members. These beliefs may be developmental at both the individual and organizational level. And because they appear to be so logical and obvious, it may be difficult to realize when one's own behavior or when faculty behavior does not match up with a particular belief.

Viewing each belief on a continuum that reflects the percentage of faculty members whose *behaviors reflect a high degree of integrity with that belief* provides the facilitation team and the faculty with a rough needs assessment of organizational receptiveness to using schoolwide action research. Or, turning the beliefs into questions, we can ask:

1. To what degree do we believe that *a collective problem-solving approach* to school renewal leads to individual professional enhancement and to a better education for our students?

2. To what degree do we *value information that keeps us regularly informed* about the health of our school community?

3. To what degree do we accept *the developmental nature of implementation*?

After staff members have identified their perceptions of how strongly each belief is operating in the school, the facilitation team can ask them to identify current behaviors and activities that reflect each belief. Part of what we want to establish is an understanding of how we would operate if these beliefs reflected normative behaviors in our school.

Here are some of the potential consequences and dilemmas relevant to each belief.

## 1. Thoughts on Collective Problem-Solving

As we begin to use action research, we find we need to modify or change the current, comfortable habits of interaction we have developed with each other, with students, and with community members. Moving to collegial, problem-solving interaction focused on collecting and using information for the common good may produce turmoil, commotion, and passive resistance among many people. This brouhaha can be expected when we disturb workplace norms and begin serious collective study of the effects of selected actions on students and on ourselves. Along with acquiring new patterns of interpersonal behavior, we may need to modify how we spend our work hours. Both the modifications themselves and the discomfort attendant to learning new patterns of behavior may generate anxiety in ourselves and our colleagues—regardless of anyone's role designation as official or unofficial leader. However, belief in our professional efficacy and in Dewey's "learning by doing" approach can help us weather the organizational turmoil and evolve healthier norms of professional interaction.

During this transition to the school as the center of inquiry, we move from isolated, private practice to public sharing of our craft and its results on students. We move from individual sustenance for educational improvement to collective nurturance. As we move through this experience, we become knowledgeable about the change process and practiced in negotiating it; we learn how to seek technical assistance or support as needed and how to add these technical skills to our on-site repertoire. We allow the energy provided by the public study of results and promising practices to fuel our commitment to enhance the education experienced by all members of our school community. We live our willingness to learn from and work with other colleagues as a unit for action. We discover that sharing increases our strength, whereas isolation diminishes it.

## 2. Thoughts About Using On-Site Information for School Improvement

Using current data to regularly monitor students' progress during the quarter or in terms of the new language arts curriculum being implemented makes great good sense in our pragmatic, information-driven culture. Yet the isolation of classrooms, and hence teachers from each other, has kept most inquiry individual and the results private. Both inquiry and its results must become public. We do not want to keep secrets from our colleagues—such as information on how successfully students are negotiating their school environment or the direct results of instruction and instructional innovations. When we keep the results of inquiry private, we isolate both ourselves and our students from the nurturance and support, both technical and social, available within our professional learning community.

Even when there is faculty consensus about the goals for school improvement, our collective action for the common good can easily fall apart when it comes to sharing the results of our actions on students. In some schools, the willingness to share how students are performing is just delayed; in other schools, it never comes into existence, thus ending the action research process. Why isn't such sharing natural to us? Maybe we believe certain information about our "clients" or the immediate results of instruction should only be shared "vertically"; or maybe we are comfortable only with sharing the results through standardized tests. Yet, as an organization of professionals with common goals, this does not make sense: it denies the individuals within the organization the legitimate opportunity to celebrate the attainment of common goals. Whatever our reasons, we often never "feel ready" to share current schoolwide data to direct the course of school improvement except through the safe distance provided by standardized tests. We must change this norm from a fear of sharing to an eagerness for sharing.

### 3. Thoughts on the Developmental Nature of Implementation

Learning the action research process will be personally and organizationally messy, but our efficiency will increase with practice and experience. By engaging in action research, we can become skilled in conducting it. But we will, as individuals and as an organization, go through beginning, intermediate, and advanced stages of competence as we learn the process. Acceptance of ourselves as learners should be obvious in our interactions with colleagues and students. We do not want to put ourselves in the trap of expecting to be "perfect" when we are beginners.

Whether the idea for action research for school improvement was generated by the school faculty, selected as a worthy tool by the school leadership team through the process of shared decision making, or selected by the central office, participating individuals appear to proceed through Fuller's (1969) and Hall and Hord's (1987) stages of concern at varying rates and with varying degrees of anxiety, knowledge, and skill—as with any innovation. Whether the focus (idea, approach, or project) of implementation is self-selected or handed down, individual and organizational responses to change seem to follow the patterns identified by Hall and Hord (1987):

- concerns unrelated to the innovation;
- informational and personal concerns related to the innovation;
- task concerns related to management; and
- impact concerns related to the benefits for students and how to make the innovation better.

The complexity of learning to work together, to study and publicly share on-site data as a school unit, and to operate as a learning community engaged in group investigation over our common work requires public commitments and collective energy for sustenance. *Just learning to work together over instruction and its immediate results appears to be a major innovation in most schools.* Be patient, while at the same time self-applying pressure and support.

So, collect data and share results, work together to select innovations for your setting, study implementation and share the results, reshape the initiative, and share implementation and results again and again.

*    *    *

Establishing these six conditions and actively tending these three beliefs will facilitate the initiation and maintenance of schoolwide action research—or most other school-based innovations, for that matter. These conditions and beliefs describe how colleagues in pursuit of a common goal work with and learn from each other. What I recommend can be summarized by this statement: *Let's structure our workplace/learning environment so we will be more likely to attain our common goals.*

The school leadership team or facilitator team needs to share these nine items with faculty members before a final decision is made to implement schoolwide action research:

### Tangible Conditions That Support Schoolwide Action Research

1. A faculty where a majority of teachers wish to change the status quo of education in their school;

2. A common public agreement about how collective decisions will be made and implemented;

3. A facilitation team willing to lead the action research process;

4. Small study groups that meet regularly;

5. A basic knowledge of the action research cycle and the rationale for its use; and

6. Someone to provide technical assistance and support.

### Intangible Beliefs That Support Schoolwide Action Research

1. To believe that a collective problem-solving approach to school renewal leads to individual professional enhancement and to a better education for our students;

2. To value information that keeps us regularly informed about the health of our learning community; and

3. To accept the developmental nature of implementation, both the technical and concerns-based aspects of using schoolwide action research.

Seeking school renewal through action research is a lot of work, but we do have a structure to follow. As Bruner reminded us in 1973, we do not have to discover everything; models can provide effective structures to support learning. Before reading Chapters 4–8 on the phases of action research, look carefully at Figure 3.3, "Quick-Start to Action Research." Imagine that you and your faculty are a large class of students engaging in cooperative learning. I'll bet you could take this abbreviated outline on the five phases of action research and begin right now!

---

**Figure 3.3**

**Quick-Start to Action Research**

ENGAGE

Phase 1.            Faculty identifies an area of interest.

Phase 2A.           Faculty, leadership team, or task force
                    identifies data to be collected immediately.

Phase 2B.           Faculty or task force collects data.

Phases 3–4.         Share the results across the faculty.
                    Compare results with perceptions.
                    Compare results with desirable/
                    future outcomes.

Phase 5.            Determine whether action is needed.
                    If yes, take short-term action immediately
                    and plan for long-term action

Remember, it's a good idea to start with existing archival data and
expand to more complex data sources during the process.

# 4
# Phase 1: Selecting
# an Area or Focus

CHAPTERS 4–8 DESCRIBE HOW TO CONDUCT SCHOOLWIDE ACTION
research. They outline the five phases of action that
successful organizations generally follow and that I advise
"first time" action research teams to use (see Figure 1.1).
The procedures, and my blunt advice about how to avoid
pitfalls, come from research on organizations engaged in
action research. My emphasis is on schoolwide or collective
action research by the entire faculties of schools.

Although making distinctions between phases is useful,
we need to keep in mind that they "roll" into one another
and that backtracking may be necessary, possibly more
than once. Take a look at Item 2 in the Appendix to get a
sense of what the cycle looks like in terms of faculty
behaviors.

If you have used the alternate route to school
accreditation, been involved in comprehensive planning
and needs assessment aimed at improving student
achievement, or taught a class in which students were
engaged in selecting a focus for their study and were
heavily involved in assessing their own progress, then this
sequence of behaviors will look familiar.

Most of the examples in these chapters assume that
there is a facilitation team, that the tasks involve
interchanges between the team and the faculty, and that
some tasks are being conducted by the team and others by
the faculty. In a small school, the entire faculty may serve as
the facilitation team.

## The Focus of Action Research

The content for the focus of schoolwide action research is student learning. The total faculty or a school leadership team identifies an area of interest for schoolwide, collective attention. This may be a problem area such as the quality of student writing or a possible problem area such as the sparsity of original prose or poetry being generated by students. Or the faculty may decide to collect some general baseline information first and then select a focus. Whatever the faculty selects for collective study and action needs to *focus primarily on what students are experiencing or have experienced*, not on what adults in the school are experiencing.

The essence of Phase 1 is organizing the faculty to examine the health of the school and to find areas where efforts can be made to improve it. Beginning the inquiry, the faculty asks the question: *What do we study?*

Common patterns for selecting an area for collective study can be classified into (1) those that are like an informal needs assessment and (2) those that are more like a formal needs assessment. I recommend that you go with the one that seems to best suit your faculty's temperament and that will more quickly marshall faculty energy toward improving students' education.

## Informal Needs Assessment

In an informal needs assessment, faculty members consider student life and achievement in their school and pick an area of collective concern. If they have consensus as a group, this area becomes their focus for study. This focus is then worded as a goal for collective action. If they do not have consensus, they need to prioritize their areas of concern.

For example, the facilitation team conducts a survey to determine faculty perceptions of the greatest areas of need. One question is enough—something like:

> What is the greatest priority for enhancing student education in our school that we can act on this year and continue with over the next few years?

Facilitation team members take the written responses and form a list of areas of concern. They give this list to faculty members for individual review followed by discussions within each study group. When the general faculty meeting is held to select a focus for schoolwide study, a brief overview of the rationale for each area should be presented. After faculty members have had an opportunity to listen and ask questions, the list can be handed out again to each faculty member. At this time they are asked to rate each area from 1 to 5, with 1 representing the greatest priority for collective attention and 5 the lowest immediate priority.

In selecting the top priority, each faculty member should ask this question: *Which area, if selected, would have the greatest benefits for our students?*

The following discussion of focus areas will make some people angry and will generate verbal flak from some of my colleagues, but here goes. The identification of a focus for schoolwide action research is the first place where things can get seriously off track because of a lack of knowledge about research on change and the research on site-based school improvement. A few simple sets of exemplars and nonexemplars of focus areas may help the facilitation team prevent this problem.

Once the faculty selects a focus area, members develop a focus statement that identifies the area of investigation and expresses it in terms of a goal for pursuit by the professional community. The list that follows includes examples of focus areas aimed directly at student learning; actually, they are collectively pursued goals. The second list includes innovations—possible routes or actions to take to attain collective goals. These innovations are aimed directly at changes in teacher behavior or materials used, not at student learning. The third list of focus areas relates to the worklife conditions of adults in the school or to student discipline. These items concern important climate variables in the school, but they move even further from a direct focus on student learning than those in the second list.

***Examples of Focus Areas.*** Here are some focus areas for collective action currently being pursued by school faculties:

- improve problem-solving skills in mathematics among all students;
- increase global literacy among all students;
- improve students' attitudes about and achievement in reading;
- improve the quality and variety of student writing;
- increase student achievement across all subject areas;
- increase student achievement and self-esteem; and
- increase the use of cooperative learning among students in all subject areas.

These items are goals for *collective study and action.* They focus on improvements in student learning. Many of the items that would go in this list look much like good, large-scale classroom behavioral objectives, and they can specify cognitive or social development. They are statements that school staff members, parents, and the community can rally around and say, "Yes! We want this for our students!"

***Examples of Innovations.*** Here are some examples of innovations. These are not focus statements to enhance student learning:

- translate whole-language strategies to all curriculum areas;
- apply literature-based instructional strategies and thematic units;
- broaden teachers' knowledge base about the teaching of science;
- integrate curriculum areas;
- develop a comprehensive plan for school improvement;
- provide staff development on implementing the new mathematics curriculum; and
- identify student learning styles.

These items are actions that may be selected to help attain collective goals. These innovations or actions are means to an end. In terms of disciplined inquiry, the faculty as members of a learning community may select them after they have formally studied how students are performing and after they have studied the research information available about these options and talked with or read about how these innovations are operating in other schools. *These innovations may then form part of the schoolwide initiative that the faculty formulates and expresses through its action plan. When faculties identify innovations as a focus instead of identifying goals for students, the school renewal process often falls out of the inquiry mode of collective problem-solving and becomes a series of activities to support the implementation of the innovation.*

If the responses turned in on the faculty survey ("What do we study?") look like items in the "innovation" list, you will need to take another step before you can make a final selection of a focus for schoolwide action research: you must translate the areas of concern into goal statements focused on student learning. Members of the facilitation team can still organize these original responses for faculty review. They classify them into groups that represent common content. Then in a faculty meeting or in study groups, colleagues are given these sets and asked to specify *in terms of student behavior* why they believe these innovations need to be implemented.

***Examples of Organizational and Social Refinements.*** Here are some examples of focus statements that relate to refining organizational structures and processes of interaction. These are not focus statements that lead directly to improved student learning.

- improve teacher morale;
- improve communication between faculty and administration;
- improve classroom management techniques;
- improve discipline throughout the school; and
- improve grade-level planning.

Each item in this list represents a worthy goal, but these statements focus more on smoothing and refining organizational and social structures and processes. They describe what we want for ourselves as adults in the workplace and on changes in the management of behaviors of persons in the building. Sometimes the facilitation team can build items such as "improve communication" and "improve grade-level planning" into the action plan developed to guide the action research process. If your faculty members generate a lot of examples that relate to school climate, your selection of actions to take in Phase 5 is especially critical.

As you study the professional literature, attend especially to those innovations that have historically paid off in terms of increased student achievement and self-esteem. You want to select an option for action that will help your faculty move as quickly as possible into "behaving and feeling like" an efficacious professional unit because of what they have accomplished with their students.

I have many reasons for elaborating on exemplars and nonexemplars of focus areas for schoolwide action research. If your collective desire is to enhance the education of your students, go with items that match the criteria for placement in the first list (focused directly on student learning), not those in the second list (innovations) or those in the third list (aimed more at organizational process and conditions). Select a focus that has strong face validity with your faculty—one behind which almost every faculty member would unite and say, "Yes, this is critically important."

## A More Formal Needs Assessment

In schoolwide action research, there are two versions of this more formal needs assessment. One version I call a *mini-formal* needs assessment; the other I call an *extensive* needs assessment. The two major discriminators of these versions are the time they consume and the quantity of information collected. Both versions generally follow Phases 1–4 of the action research cycle: identification of areas to explore; collection of information; and its organization, analysis, and interpretation. The process concludes with a status report on the areas explored. This information is then used to identify a focus for collective study and action.

In the mini-formal assessment, school faculty members study student information currently available in their school files. They look at indicators of students' academic and social progress within the school or at the cumulative history of schooling on students. For example, How many students are currently academically and socially successful using the current school criteria of success? How many students have been retained one time or more and what are the grades of these students right now? Who is being referred and why? Finding the answers to these questions generally takes one to four months. The mini-formal assessment operates as a very fast version of Phases 2–4 of the action research cycle. The faculty uses the results of this assessment to select a priority focus area for collective action.

In the extensive, formal needs assessment, Phases 1–4 of the action research process become an extended needs assessment for determining the focus. The assessment would have a broad focus and would investigate the current state of students' cognitive and social learning across all student experiences sanctioned by and within the school. When the information from the assessment has been summarized and presented, faculty members use it to select their focus for collective action.

## Guidelines and Recommendations for Phase 1

These guidelines on the selection of a focus for collective action are based on more than my experiences in schools conducting action research. The research on change and innovation that has accumulated over the past fifty years is clear on several points:

1. Successful schools focus on student learning as a collective mission.

2. Instructional and curricular innovations are essential to school improvement, but they *serve* the central goal of enhancing student learning.

3. Organizational norms and processes need to change in many schools to support a healthier learning community for staff members. These changes in relationships, behaviors, and work tasks are exciting, but if they become the operational focus for school renewal, enhanced education for students and adults may be submerged.

I recommend use of the mini-formal and the informal needs assessments for publicly selecting a focus for collective study and action. My reasons for this are that when either of these is well done, the faculty is able to move into selecting options and taking action to affect their area of concern or focus in a relatively short amount of time.

With the extensive formal needs assessment, faculties generally take a year before they are ready to select a priority focus. During this year of very hard work, collective energy for renewal often dissipates; and faculty members feel nothing has been accomplished. So far, I have not seen any advantages for students or for the total adult learning community of using the extensive formal needs assessment over using a well-conducted mini-formal or informal needs assessment.

Here are a few "rule of thumb" criteria the facilitation team or faculty can use to assess the focus statement:

• The focus statement affects lifetime behavior and quality of life for students.

• The mission is often something you can involve students in attaining—it is in their interest and requires their collaboration.

• The focus area has face validity for school staff, parents, and the community.

• It directly relates to the mission of the school.

• Most citizens in our society would agree that it directly supports the purposes for which schools exist.

# 5
# Phase 2: Collecting Data

YOUR SELECTION OF A FOCUS AREA AND A CLEAR, SHARED STATEMENT of it are important first steps in action research. Next, if it has not begun already, is the data-gathering phase. Somebody (task force, facilitation team, or entire school staff) decides what data will be collected in the area under investigation and how the data will be collected, from whom, and how often. Collection of baseline data is only the beginning—*action research is a formative study of progress*, requiring regular and frequent data collection so that changes and trends can be seen. For vital areas of interest, such as the effect of the new mathematics curriculum on students' achievement and attitude in mathematics or grades being made by at-risk students, data collection may occur as often as biweekly for a year or more.

## What Data Do We Collect?

The first task in the data-collection phase is to decide what data will be collected. This decision has two substantive aspects: (1) What data do we collect about the learner? and (2) What data do we collect about the learning environment provided by the school? First, let's consider data about the student as learner.

The big question is, *What sources will provide the faculty with information about student learning?* How are students doing in the academic, social, and personal domains of our focus area?

In the academic domain, we need to find out how well students are learning how to learn. For example, are they learning how to explore the world of mathematics and use the concepts of the discipline to solve new problems, and are they learning how to teach themselves mathematics? In terms of productivity in mathematics, what do grades indicate about student performance, and what do standardized test scores indicate?

In the social domain, we need to know whether students know how to use the social system for support as learners. In the personal domain, we need information on how students feel about mathematics, and how they feel about themselves as students of mathematics. What is their academic self-esteem in relation to mathematics?

As the faculty inquires into student learning in their area of interest and gathers information in response to these questions, they will use student data from a variety of sources.

Once the faculty has identified data sources that provide a picture of how students are performing, then faculty members need to develop a picture of how their school influences student learning in their focus area. The big data-collection question here is, *What sources will provide information about the learning environment of the school?* Here are a few questions a faculty can ask as they generate possible sources of information.

- How *do* schools affect learning?
- What experiences are sanctioned and provided by our school as an organization to enhance student learning?
- What is happening in curriculum and instruction—or, more specifically, what are we teaching and how are we teaching it?
- What do *our actions* look like?
- What are we doing as a learning community?

Again, keeping the collective attention firmly on what the faculty can control and on what has been shown to pay off in terms of student learning, the faculty and facilitation team will need to select multiple data sources as they inquire into the experiences they are providing for students.

During the first action research cycle, the question of what data we collect to inform us about student learning is primary. In fact, a complete cycle can be conducted to answer this question, followed immediately by a second cycle, during which the faculty looks at the experiences the school provides for students in the focus area. When student learning and the experience of schooling are investigated separately, the first two cycles function as needs assessment: the first cycle assesses student learning in the focus area, and the second cycle assesses the learning environment in the focus area. However, if the faculty spends too much time studying on-site data without taking any action to improve student learning, the energy of the faculty can dissipate. My recommendation is to gather information on some aspects of both these questions during the first action research cycle: What is the status of student learning? and What is the status of schooling in our focus area? During recurring cycles of Phases 2–4, the faculty can collect additional information in response to each question.

### Identifying Sources of Data for Action Research

What sources of information will help us develop a schoolwide response to the two major data-collection questions—how are students performing in our area of interest and what experiences of schooling might affect that performance?

The facilitation team and faculty seek data sources that will provide an accurate picture of the student behavior they wish to influence. Where do they start? To get action research and collective study going, it's a good idea to *use existing archival data sources immediately, conventional data sources next, and then more inventive and elaborate data sources* (see Figure 5.1). These three categories of data sources provide a useful framework to school faculties as they develop their data-collection schedule. The categories serve as a bank of ideas; they can stimulate reflections about why we collect information from a particular source; and they can serve as a filter to prevent a data-collection overload that overwhelms the faculty, thus preventing collective action.

Think about these three sources on a continuum, with existing sources at one end and inventive sources at the other. The depth of information increases as one moves across the continuum from existing sources to inventive sources. Generally, in data collection, organization, and analysis, the time investment increases as one moves from existing to conventional and from conventional to inventive.

---

### Figure 5.1
### Sources of Data for Action Research

| Existing Archival Sources | Conventional Sources | Inventive Sources |
|---|---|---|
| Student grades | Surveys | Exhibits |
| Attendance | Simple interviews | Portfolios |
| Referrals | Number of books read | Expositions |
| Retentions | Writing samples | Videotapes |
| Number/percentage of students in special programs | Variety of materials used | |
| Standardized test results | Observations | |
| | Journals | |

However, information from one category is not any "better" than information from another category. The tricky decisions have to do with what sort of information is provided by sources within each category and when we need this information.

**1. *Existing Archival Sources.*** Existing sources of data are those items currently available in the files or archives of the school or of individual staff members. Data about the school population can be gathered and organized directly from these records. Some examples are student grades, discipline referrals, standardized test results, and demographics. The collection of data from these sources requires little effort and time from the faculty, but information from them provides the faculty with an immediate picture of the educational climate of the school.

Within the category of existing, archival sources are several indicators of student behavior that we call *fate-control variables*. These indicators of student behavior are so critical to student learning that each member of the school faculty needs to have a clear, schoolwide picture of them, because they provide a rough map of the academic and social climate of the school. Variables such as attendance, referrals, grades, and courses taken indicate *how many students are present or absent for instruction, how many students are moving successfully or unsuccessfully through school, and how many students are making use of the educational opportunities being offered.* We call them fate-control variables because they have so much influence on the fate of each student who enters our school.

Faculties have been amazed at what they have discovered when they looked at their fate-control variables. Here are a few dramatic examples: one-third of all students being sent to in-house suspension were sent for tardiness (yes, they were "housed," but they were absent from instruction); 9th grade males were absent twice as much as any other group; no African-American females have graduated from our school in the last five years; more students are making *D*'s and *F*'s in our Vocational/Business Education classes than in our advanced academic courses; one-fourth of the students coming to us from the 8th grade are over-age and lacking in basic reading and mathematics skills; over the past three years, approximately one-half of the students who took Spanish I did not take Spanish II; approximately 90 percent of the 1st graders who enter our Chapter 1/Prep Program are still in Chapter 1 five, four, three . . . years later.

For some reason, looking at grades as a source of data can be uncomfortable, especially at the middle and high school levels. As soon as grade distributions are presented, and sometimes before, faculty members disparage grades as a data source. Here are some usual comments: "Grades are not valid sources." "Grades do not represent what our students have learned." "Grades for the same level of performance vary from teacher to teacher."

This is my first response to these comments: At the most elemental level, whether the grades are valid, what they represent, and how much they vary does not matter. As long as grades are being used by the school, they are a primary source of data about student learning in that school. Grades are the currency of success in many schools. They control whether a student moves from one grade level to the next, from one course to another, and in many cases into which "track" she will be placed for several years and into which university or technical school she will be accepted.

My second response to these comments is a combination of reminders and questions: We are engaged in inquiry. Grades are one source of knowledge for use in our collective inquiry. If this is the way we feel about grades, how must students feel? Maybe our system of assigning grades is something we will want to explore in Phase 5, Taking Action. Maybe some teachers are using a criterion-referenced system of assigning grades, and others are using a norm-referenced method. This may be an area for group investigation. However, as long as we assign grades to our learners, we use grades as a source of information on the learners and the learning environment of our school.

The data for these fate-control variables are from existing sources; therefore, they are easily available for collective study. The faculty needs to look at them early because they provide a rich source of information about the educational climate of the school.

Now we move on to data sources that provide us with additional information about the behaviors and attitudes of our students, of ourselves as faculty members, and of parents or other community members.

**2. *Conventional Sources.*** Conventional sources of data are items that require communication, observation, or follow-up with members of the population and that often require instrumentation to standardize the information collected. Therefore, the collection of data from these sources requires the selection or development of data-collection instruments. Examples of conventional data sources are surveys, interviews, observations, samples of student work, journals, and logs of performance. Information from these sources can be easily acquired and organized in a brief span of time.

With existing data sources, we gather information from school archives and staff records; with conventional data sources, we gather information directly from individuals, from samples of their work, and from documents that require study. We seek information from these sources when we want to know more about the behaviors and attitudes of students in our area of interest.

When you are developing your action plan and its data-collection schedule, you want to include a balance of behavioral and perceptual data sources. Behavioral data sources provide the faculty with information about what a person is doing or has done. Behavioral sources include logs that indicate the number of books students have read; samples of student writing; observations of students at work; and, for the faculty, logs of types of writing elicited, samples of lessons, and descriptions of how concepts are presented. Perceptual sources provide the faculty with information about the feelings, opinions, and values of a person. Perceptual sources include surveys, questionnaires, and interviews.

*Avoid overreliance on perceptual data sources.* I am addressing the overuse of surveys and attitudinal measures specifically because it is so common. I have seen faculties select excellent student learning goals, then (1) identify as their primary data source a survey of themselves with student achievement and attitude about school as the content or (2) develop and administer three long surveys to parents, students, and staff. The goals focused on student learning, yet no behavioral data on student learning were collected. Part of the faculty's picture of student learning was missing in both cases because the data did not include any direct indicators of student performance, such as grades, quality of writing, skill in problem-solving, or standardized test results. Using surveys or questionnaires to collect perceptions about what is and beliefs about how oneself or others operate provides useful information to pour into our decision-making funnel; however, what individuals and groups are actually doing (the behavioral part of the picture) provides even more useful information.

Here are two key reminders that can improve the quality of data collection immediately: collect behavioral data whenever possible (see examples of "Inventive" data on science and the section on using multiple sources of data for language arts instruction) and keep your initial surveys short and of high quality. When collecting perceptual data, use available surveys, or questions from them, if possible, or carefully design three or four questions that will provide high-quality information related to the collective goal. Field test these questions on friends in another school, in your neighborhood, or in classes you are taking. Find out if the questions will provide the information that your faculty is seeking.

Comparing the results of perceptual data with the results of behavioral data may be a rich source of information for the individual and for the faculty. There can be discrepancies between what people believe they are doing and what their performance indicates. For example, data summarized from a questionnaire indicated that teachers were providing explicit instruction in writing expository prose to their classes as total groups and to individuals within each class; data from student surveys agreed with this perception of writing instruction. Yet, when these teachers and their students kept a log of instructional tasks in Weeks 4 and 6 of the second quarter, very little explicit instruction was provided. When student teachers served as recorders in Weeks 3 and 5, they documented little explicit instruction in writing. As teachers discussed this discrepancy, they made comments like these: "Maybe, when we answered this series of items, we were thinking about the amount of time we provided for student writing." "On these, I was thinking about all the tasks I assign students that relate to reading and responding to short-answer questions in their textbooks."

This is one example of many I could name; you probably have your own to add. These discrepancies between our perceptions and assumptions and our behaviors may be far more common than we would like to believe. Action research allows us to confront these discrepancies. We confront them through the study of our student and school data and through the study of the professional literature offered by our colleagues.

*3. Inventive Data Sources.* Inventive data sources are usually examples of products or performance. We use these sources when we want even more in-depth information about performance than we can gain from existing and conventional sources. For student products and performances, these items are directly linked to the learning goals of the school; their purpose is to provide the student and the larger school community with an accurate and more direct measure of what students know and how they think, as individuals. These items require the development of criteria for analyzing the products and performances and a greater investment of faculty time in the collection, organization, and analysis phases. Examples of inventive data sources related to student products and performances include portfolios, exhibits, and videotapes. Many of us associate these data sources with "authentic assessment."

For collecting data about faculty products and performances, the sources used are directly linked to the goals of the schoolwide initiative; their purpose is to provide the individual and the faculty with an accurate and more direct (than surveys and perceptual data) measure of staff performance in terms of the actions or innovations being implemented. Examples of inventive data sources related to staff products and performances include units and materials developed to support an instructional strategy and videotapes of instruction.

## A Scenario on Using Different Sources of Data

Let's say that a high school faculty is concerned about student performance in science. First, the faculty needs to consider existing data sources, things that are available in the files—such as student grades in physical science, biology, physics, chemistry, and so forth; how many students are taking science gatekeeper courses that affect their admission to colleges and universities; how many students take only one gatekeeper course, fail it, and drop into another "track"; whether any group of students is underrepresented in the gatekeeper courses and, if yes, to what extent. The faculty also looks at standardized test scores in science from locally administered general achievement batteries and disaggregates these data by groups of concern, such as male/female or Hispanic/African-American/Caucasian.

Second, the faculty might consider conventional sources for generating additional data. For this high school initiative in science, the faculty might consider surveys of students' attitudes toward science, interviews focused on students' academic self-esteem in relation to science, interviews focused on how students prefer to learn, an inventory of the variety and types of materials used in science courses, teacher and student logs of the instructional approaches used in science classes and

student responses to the instruction offered, and interviews on how students use science concepts at home or in their after-school work. Also, the faculty may want to involve students as something more than "subjects." Students engaged in the data-collection process (or action research process) are provided with rich learning opportunities in sociology, statistics, journalism, and other disciplines; students also provide additional energy and human resources through their involvement in and support of the "schoolwide" initiative.

Eventually, this high school faculty might consider more inventive, creative sources that relate to the students' abilities to think and perform like scientists, such as presentations of individual or group research projects, science exhibits, videotapes of students working as an investigative team forming and checking their hypotheses, and structured assessment activities designed to assess goals in science that are most highly valued within this high school learning community.

## Using Multiple Sources of Data

Now that we have reviewed more than you ever wanted to know about sources of data for schoolwide action research, let's take a look at the value of using more than one source of information. The facilitation team and faculty *select multiple sources of data* for collective study to develop an accurate picture of how students are performing and of what students are experiencing. Through these multiple sources, the faculty seeks greater knowledge and understanding of the learner and the learning environment.

This process can be called *data triangulation*—the use of a variety of data sources to study our focus area. We use these multiple sources of information to develop a comprehensive perspective. Although a single data source may provide us with an abundance of information, we would rarely wish to end our inquiry into our area of interest based on this sole source. As we select data sources and build their collection into our action plan, we want to look at our fate-control variables, and we want to look at behavioral and perceptual sources that relate to our focus area.

Frequently, information we analyze from one data source will lead us to seek information from another source. This is often the case when we look at information from existing data sources or at information from conventional data sources, such as restricted-choice surveys and instruments with Likert scales. Each source has its strengths and weaknesses. By using multiple sources, we can strengthen the clarity and depth of our understanding while we minimize the weaknesses of any single source.

Let's look at an example. An elementary school faculty, concerned about students' low scores in reading comprehension on standardized achievement tests and about the numbers of upper-elementary students who expressed negative feelings about reading, selected language arts as its area of interest for schoolwide improvement. Faculty members knew that the results of standardized tests administered once a year were not adequate to measure the effects they desired on student skill in language, nor were the results useful for guiding immediate action to improve student learning.

The faculty requested that the facilitation team identify data sources that would yield results to serve three major purposes: (1) to provide baseline information on students' language arts communication skills and attitudes; (2) to guide immediate action at the school, classroom, and student level; and (3) to assess progress over time. Consequently, the facilitation team identified eight data sources to use in determining the effects of their initiative on students: student grades (Satisfactory/Needs Improvement/Unsatisfactory and A/B/C/D/F) in language arts, student scores on the reading and language sections of statewide-administered standardized achievement tests, media center checkout (number of books), student and classroom logs of number of books read outside of school, student and classroom logs of number of pieces written, writing samples from students, parent surveys of students' attitudes toward reading, and the number of books students submitted to the Parents and Teachers Association for publication each month. Other data sources—such as more elaborate language portfolios, videotapes of student storytelling, miscue analysis records, reading records for parents, and anecdotal records—were considered by the team but not selected for collective use at this time;

however, any teacher or study team could collect additional data if they wished.

To provide information about the learning environment, the facilitation team and faculty decided to gather information about writing instruction and about the quality of the curriculum materials being used. Teachers kept logs of the types of writing they elicited from students (expository, narrative, persuasive, and "free writing"), how much time they spent providing explicit instruction in writing as a craft, and the types of instructional strategies they were using for writing instruction. Study-group teams began to analyze the curriculum materials—textbooks, activity books, computer software, worksheets, and other supplementary materials—for their usefulness in terms of developing skilled writers. As faculty members discussed the results of their data-gathering efforts, before any schoolwide "interpretation of results," they suggested many actions and changes.

The screen for identifying data for collection is simple if the faculty has identified its collective goal. *Goals set the parameters for selecting data sources that will provide information relevant to student performance and attitudes.* Here is a quick check on the data-collection process. Look at your action plan: If all or most of the data sources identified provide information about *teacher* behaviors or perceptions or about *parent* behaviors or perceptions— with few or no data sources that provide information about *student* performance and perceptions—revise your plan. Focus more on gathering data on students and balance the collection of data across the three role groups.

The use of multiple sources of information adds greater complexity to our collective inquiry; however, it is a complexity that yields a clearer understanding of the learner and the learning environment. Figure 5.2 provides a smorgasbord of data sources. You can use this list of possibilities as a resource list or as a springboard for generating what to collect to inform the faculty about the life students are experiencing in your school.

**Figure 5.2**

**Smorgasbord of Internal Data Sources**

**Existing Archival Sources**

- Attendance rates of students and teachers—by school, grade level.
- Retention rate/promotion rate—by school, grade level, teacher, and particular groups [e.g., male/female, race/ethnicity, high/middle/low socioeconomic status (SES)].
- Retainees—number and percentage of students at each grade level who have been retained once, twice, or more.
- Discipline referrals—by school, grade level, classroom, particular groups.
- Dropout rate—by school, grade level, classroom, particular groups.
- Suspension rates—by school, grade level, classroom, particular groups.
- Number and percentage positive (and negative) parent communications—by school, grade level.
- Membership in parent/teacher organization (PTO) (percent parents); attendance at PTO meetings.
- Grade distribution in science, math, social studies, etc.—by SES, race/ethnicity, gender.
- Standardized test data (Iowa Tests of Basic Skills, criterion-referenced tests, tests of academic proficiency). Use raw scores, if possible, for comparison.
- Number and percentage of students "labeled" as learning disabled, Chapter 1, gifted, etc.—by school, grade level. May also want to look at number of years students have been in specific programs, such as Chapter 1.
- Number and percentage of students participating in school-sponsored organizations (e.g., Distributive Education Clubs of America, Future Business Leaders of America, Student Council, Yearbook Club, Drama Club, etc.)—by school, grade level, classroom, academic "track," particular groups.

---

**Figure 5.2—*continued***

**Conventional and Inventive Sources**

• Number of books read by students and by school staff—by school, grade level, class.

• Library use—by school, grade level.

• Writing samples.

• Teacher journals—focused on the schoolwide initiative.

• Student journals—focused on the schoolwide initiative (e.g., 5 minutes spent writing about today's class).

• Student attitude surveys about reading or math, followed by interviews.

• Videotapes of students working in cooperative groups.

• Videotapes of students solving math problems.

• Students' written descriptions of math problems.

• Math journals (students draw pictures or write equations for word problems, or vice versa).

• Number of hours allocated to formal student assessment, for state standardized tests and for end-of-unit/level tests—by grade level, class.

• Records of peer observations or observation journals

• Videotapes of teachers using new teaching strategies or new materials, such as math manipulations.

• Concerns survey—beginning of year, midpoint, end, etc.

• Interviews about schoolwide initiative—when surveys do not provide enough information.

• Minutes from follow-up meetings after staff development sessions.

• Measures of level of implementation—fidelity to models used in staff development.

• Shared-governance journals.

• Minutes from shared governance, council, task force meetings.

• Nature and amount of in-school assistance in curriculum implementation, data analysis, staff development from central office or regional service agencies.

• Nature of assistance, numbers of, and amount of time contributed by volunteer parents or community members—by school, grade level.

• Number of hours teachers and administrators participate in required staff development activities and in voluntary professional development activities—by school, grade level.

(*continued on next page*)

---

**Figure 5.2**—*continued*

**Document Review**

• Analyze local board of education policies, rules, and regulations pertinent to the school's instructional initiative.

• Analyze local curriculum guides for information pertinent to the school's instructional initiative.

• Analyze district and state standardized tests and their accompanying technical and content manuals and the numerous reports sent back to the school district for information pertinent to the school's instructional initiative.

• Survey accreditation reports for information pertinent to the school's instructional initiative.

*Note:* Remember to assign a number or code to "anonymous" information, such as parents' attitude surveys, so that you can compare them over several years.

### Seeking Resources and Technical Assistance.

Several resources that are particularly useful to school teams as they think about data collection and instrument design include:

- *Qualitative Evaluation Methods* (Patton 1980);
- *Asking Questions: A Practical Guide to Questionnaire Design* (Sudman and Bradburn 1982);
- *Qualitative Data Analysis: A Sourcebook of New Methods* (Miles and Huberman 1984); and
- *The Collection, Analysis, and Use of Monitoring and Evaluation Data* (Casley and Kumar 1988), a World Bank publication.

Although many of the examples provided by Casley and Kumar (1988) are from agriculture, the structures offered for gathering information, analyzing and understanding the data gathered, and organizing and presenting results are applicable to most inquiries involving people and events.

In the data-collection phase, many faculties find technical assistance to be useful in identifying, selecting, or developing instruments such as attitudinal surveys, interview schedules, scales for analyzing writing samples, assessments of particular types of mathematical problem-solving skills, and so forth. However, if existing data are available, begin collecting those immediately while seeking assistance and acquiring more sophisticated sources. A staff brainstorming session will usually generate multiple sources of data concerning an area of interest; however, for a general topic not yet defined through specific behaviors, such as "improve student self-esteem," technical assistance might be useful for rapidly generating data sources and analysis possibilities. This assistance might be found at the local district office, through an intermediate service agency, from a nearby university, or through a consulting firm.

## How Do We Collect the Data?

The response to this question is "as simply as possible." Some of it is already stored in computers and file drawers; some of it has to be requested and collected from students, staff members, and parents. As the facilitation team and faculty determine what they will collect, they move almost simultaneously to *how* they will collect and organize the data. Simple forms and logs are extremely useful. Faculty members need to know exactly what information to turn in and how it should be organized, especially if it includes information from a group or from the whole class. It's often a good idea for members of the facilitation team to pilot the data-gathering forms in their classrooms to discover if modifications are needed and to assist them in planning for Phase 3, data organization. See Items 3a, 3b, and 4 in the Appendix for samples of forms that have been used by school faculties for collecting data.

## From Whom Do We Collect Data?

The decision to be made here revolves around this question: "For our faculty to have an accurate picture of performance relative to our goal, how much data need to be collected and from whom?" Think back to your statistics courses and recall *how to sample from a population and when you would want to do this*.

For some purposes, you want to collect data from all students in your school, such as amounts of outside-of-school reading or grades. For other purposes, you may want to use a sample. For example, you may want to interview a random sample of six males and six females from each grade level (1–6) whose reading logs indicate a high level of reading, as well as six males and six females from each grade level whose reading logs indicate that they are not reading anything outside of school. Or, in relation to grades, you may want to interview a similar sample of the population—high achievers and low achievers this time—and ask whether they are successful in school and why. For taking a picture of classroom instruction that relates to your collective goal, you may want all teachers to keep a log of tasks and class assignments, accompanied by observations of a random sample of teachers.

The question remains: When do you collect data from everyone and when do you take a sample? You take a sample when it will give you all the information you want. My own rule of thumb is to gather data from the *whole* student population when we are concerned about each student's performance and when we are going to use the results as formative information for goal attainment. For example, how many students know their basic number facts, how much are students reading, how much are students writing, how many students are being referred and for what purpose? And we gather data from the whole faculty when we need a complete picture of what is being provided in the learning environment and when we are going to use the results to make decisions about implementation; staff development; and the use of time, energy, materials, and other resources. For example, for which mathematical concepts are we using manipulables and how often, how often are students engaging in empirical problem solving, how much time are we allocating to explicit instruction in writing, and what modes of written discourse are we eliciting and how often?

We gather data from a *sample* of the population when we need to increase our understanding while limiting our expenditure of time and energy. After reviewing the results gathered from the larger population, we can take a systematic or random sample of students or teachers from each grade level and probe for more information and greater understanding of behaviors, feelings, or attitudes related to our focus area. Common data-gathering methods used for depth of understanding include interviews, observations, shadow studies, and document review. Often, when faculties study the fate-control variables (grades, referrals, etc.) and results from conventional data sources (surveys, logs, etc.), they encounter puzzling responses or patterns. These responses and patterns often stimulate the faculty to seek more information—and this is a prime time to sample.

Once the facilitation team and faculty have identified the data they will collect, selected or designed instruments and forms to use in collecting these data, and decided from whom these data will be collected, data collection begins. In the early stages, it is especially critical for the facilitation team to look at this information as soon as it comes in. Find out if a picture is being provided, whether the data "appear" to make sense, and if any glitches occur in the data-collection instruments or procedures. If changes in the data-collection process need to be made, involve the faculty in making them or inform the faculty of the changes if that is more appropriate or if the changes are minor.

## How Often Do We Collect Data?

Now we move from what data to collect to the issue of how often. Data focused on students' academic and social learning and attitudes and collected *at appropriate intervals* can provide a reasonably accurate picture of the effects of our actions on students. Although both short and long intervals can be appropriate, the most common error made when specifying a data-collection plan is to make the intervals too wide, such as quarterly or yearly, when more frequent collection would be better for assessing progress and guiding actions. The following example addresses some of the issues of "appropriate frequency."

A school faculty selected "improving students' written language" as their schoolwide initiative. They defined the intent of their initiative through four major effects on students: (1) increase in amounts of original prose and poetry, (2) increase in quality of student writing, (3) increase in positive student attitudes about writing, and (4) increase understanding about how prose is crafted for the audience or reader. For the first effect, amount of writing, the faculty collected data weekly. Without immediate data on amounts of writing being solicited from students, the faculty could not select appropriate actions to take on the other three effects—quality, attitude, and the writing/reading connection.

In looking at their initial results, these faculty members were surprised at how few writing opportunities they were providing their students. (During the first six weeks, as this faculty collected their baseline data on writing quantity, just its attention to the problem worked to increase amounts of student writing.) To assess schoolwide progress on students' effects in (2) writing quality, (3) attitude, and (4) understanding of the reading/writing connection, the faculty selected data-collection intervals that ranged from six weeks to one school year. Data sources included student writing samples administered using standard writing prompts and scored using a standard criterial writing scale (12 weeks), student interviews (2 items, 6 weeks) and parent interviews (4 items, 12 weeks), student attitude questionnaires (5 items, beginning and end of year), parent questionnaires (3 items, beginning and end of year), and videotapes of student writing conferences (approximately 6 weeks). For interviews and videotapes, the faculty identified a sample of students and parents.

As you may have noticed, I have no formula or easy "rule of thumb" to help in answering the question of how often to collect data. Yet, when specifying data-collection intervals, many school faculties seem to set themselves up for failure. They set collection schedules at quarterly or yearly intervals. These lengthy intervals are appropriate for some sources and types of data and inappropriate for others. My best advice is only common sense. Remember that schoolwide action research is both formative assessment and collective inquiry; as such, the data collected provide information about student performance and information about the learning environment supporting that performance. The information derived from these data is used to guide faculty decisions; therefore, the data-collection intervals must occur frequently enough to inform the faculty of progress and to support decisions for action.

# Who Owns the Data?

*Data collected around a schoolwide initiative belong to the entire school staff.* Individuals do not collect these data for other persons—not for a designated in-school task force, a school leadership or facilitation team, a principal, or district office personnel. They belong, at a minimum, to each individual teacher collecting the data and to all faculty members. Acceptance of the value of collecting information about what students are experiencing on-site and personal ownership of the data-collection process are important in building a problem-solving community. Avoiding ownership of data collected around schoolwide, faculty-approved areas of interest subtly allows rejection of responsibility for the results.

Although the data must belong to everyone, however, someone or some group of persons such as a facilitation team must take initial responsibility for monitoring data collection until it becomes normative behavior.

### Guidelines and Recommendations for Phase 2

As you read the following list of key actions that support the data-collection phase of schoolwide action research, try to recall why each action was recommended:

- Use multiple data sources.
- Collect existing archival data immediately, then move to conventional and inventive data sources.
- Collect data regularly.
- Seek technical assistance if needed.
- Promote collective ownership of data.
- Monitor data collection until it becomes normative.

Remember, in schoolwide action research, we are engaging in inquiry, in formative assessment of our practice and its effects; we are not engaged in a terminal activity nor in summative evaluation. In Phases 2–4, we are developing a picture of how our students are performing and of what we are providing them as a total learning community. Our purpose for developing this picture is to use it to create another picture that we like better. As we identify and implement actions that will create this new picture, we continue our study of how these actions influence student learning and how they influence the educational environment of the school.

When the facilitation team or faculty looks over the data-collection methods listed in the schoolwide action plan, they want to make a final check (1) for congruence between the schoolwide goal and the data sources identified, (2) for the use of multiple data sources to clarify the picture being developed, and 3) for the frequency of collection so that data gathered can be used to inform current practice as well as future actions. Ask, "Have we collected data that match the behaviors indicated in our collective goal and that provide our faculty with an accurate picture of school life relevant to that goal?" And, "Have we collected behavioral data about what is being done and what is not being done, about who is performing at a high level and who is not, about who is participating and who is not participating, and about how people feel and perceive their experiences?" As these data come in, you roll into the next phase of action research, organizing data.

# 6
# Phase 3:
# Organizing Data

HOW DO WE SHARE WHAT WE ARE GATHERING? THE FACILITATION
team, a task force group, or the faculty will make decisions
about how the data will be organized so that the clearest
and richest picture of the area of interest or initiative is
communicated to the faculty. The methods of organization
used should make these data easy to share with the total
school staff and with small groups, such as grade-level
teams, team leaders, department heads, and study groups.
Because of the formative nature of action research, the data
should be organized to facilitate comparison of results from
one time to the next, making it easy to determine whether
progress has been made.

## Quantitative Data—Handling Numbers

Simply counting instances, events, and artifacts
provides abundant information about how students are
responding to or have responded to the experiences offered
to them under the auspices of public school education.
Organizing the data—counting instances or events—
and displaying the results in charts with numbers and
percentages; in simple frequency tables; or in tables with
mean, median, and range—arranged by class, grade level,
and school yields ample information for directing
immediate and long-term action. If there is concern about a
particular segment of the school population, the staff may
decide to compare these general profiles of effects with a
profile of effects that includes only data from this portion of
the population.

The following two examples illustrate some of the ways school faculties have organized data relevant to their collective goal.

***Disaggregating Data.*** Let's first consider existing data sources such as student grades, referrals, and standardized test results. These data need to be organized so that we can determine if there are group differences among learners in our school—such as differences in success rates between girls and boys, among various ethnic groups, and among socioeconomic levels. Or are success rates approximately the same? The answers to these questions help faculty members identify problems and provide them with information that guides action.

At the middle school and high school levels, we can also look for differences in student success rates among departments. I have observed heated professional discussions as some of these questions were answered. Uproar occurs over issues of teacher autonomy versus student equity. Although these confrontations may make us uncomfortable regardless of our position on the issue, they may also lead to a healthier learning community. As Sizer (1991) reminds us, "To pretend that serious restructuring can be done without honest confrontation is a cruel illusion." Questions of serious educational significance and student equity arise when members of one department apply a criterion-referenced approach to grades in their courses and members of another department apply a norm-referenced approach to grading. So, in some courses all students could make *A*'s if they attained the course objectives, whereas in other courses there would always be some *D*'s and *F*'s. Looking at grade distributions across departments, you might think one department had a different student population from the other departments.

The data from Xandia High School (Figure 6.1) show numbers of in-school suspensions (ISH) and out-of-school suspensions (SUS), disaggregated by grade level and by number of suspensions acquired by any student serving a suspension (from one to five). By looking at the discipline incidents that resulted in suspensions and organizing the incidents by reason, we discover that a large proportion of the suspensions were due to unexcused absences and tardies. Had these data not been disaggregated, it would not have been as apparent that the total number of offenses decrease as we look from 10th, to 11th, to 12th grade. Nor would the number of students who simply served one suspension have been as apparent.

## Figure 6.1
## Xandia High School Suspensions (780 Students)

### First Semester In-School Suspensions (IHS)

|       | Grade 10 | Grade 11 | Grade 12 | Total |
|-------|----------|----------|----------|-------|
| IHS1  | 458      | 265      | 110      | 833   |
| IHS2  | 15       | 1        | 0        | 16    |
| IHS3  | 7        | 5        | 0        | 12    |
| IHS4  | 5        | 0        | 0        | 5     |
| IHS5  | 0        | 0        | 0        | 0     |
| Total | 485      | 271      | 110      | 866   |

### First Semester Out-of-School Suspensions (SUS)

|       | Grade 10 | Grade 11 | Grade 12 | Total |
|-------|----------|----------|----------|-------|
| SUS1  | 23       | 39       | 9        | 71    |
| SUS2  | 3        | 2        | 0        | 5     |
| SUS3  | 16       | 6        | 4        | 26    |
| SUS4  | 0        | 0        | 0        | 0     |
| SUS5  | 1        | 0        | 1        | 2     |
| Total | 43       | 47       | 14       | 104   |

### First Semester Discipline Incidents
### (Reasons for ISH and SUS)

| | | | |
|---|---|---|---|
| 12 | Abusive behavior to peers | 1 | Smoking |
| 5 | Cheating | 1 | Sexually offensive behavior |
| 3 | Willful disobedience of administrator | 6 | Safety rule violation |
| 140 | Disruptive behavior | 9 | Theft |
| 13 | Eating in unauthorized areas | 225 | Unexcused absence |
| 26 | Fighting | 8 | No book or needed material |
| 2 | Forgery of school official | 282 | Unexcused tardy |
| 30 | Forgery of sponsor | 6 | Vandalism |
| 152 | Insubordination | 33 | Vulgarity, profanity |
| 52 | Leaving class without permission | 30 | No show to administrator's detention |
| 11 | Offensive behavior to teacher | | |
| 11 | Possession of prohibited item | 55 | No show to teacher's detention |

As the high school delved into these simple data, faculty members discovered two items as a collaborative community that were not as apparent to them from the perspective of a single classroom: (1) the penalty for being absent or late from class was more time out of class, and (2) the school had a group of about 30 students who were "regular" offenders. As a result of their collective confrontation with these data, the school faculty made a drive at reducing tardies and absences, thus reducing the amount of lost instructional time for many students. They also moved beyond these existing data and sought to expand their information through interviews and conferences with the small group of frequent offenders. They were determined to figure out how to engage these students in the educational opportunities provided at Xandia.

*Looking at Subgroups.* For data from conventional sources, such as student reading logs and responses to restricted-response surveys, the same process of looking at the performance of the population as a whole, then looking at subgroups, can help identify problems and generate questions that need to be answered before the picture is clarified. For example, one question on a high school survey asked students if they wanted to reinstate study hall. Most 9th and 10th grade students, many 11th grade students, and some 12th grade students responded "yes." Because this was a question with the sharpest difference across grade levels, the faculty decided to conduct interviews using a stratified random sample of students. General findings as the faculty analyzed the interview responses were that 9th and 10th graders felt they needed the time to work on assignments whereas 12th graders were not as concerned, were participating in off-campus work experiences, or were accumulating electives that would help them in college.

Lezotte (in Sparks 1993, p. 20) reminds us that disaggregation of student outcome data is "critical," "infrequently done," and "the best tool that I know of to help educators describe the problem." If we believe that all students can learn and that quality instruction leads to student learning, then the disaggregation of data can help us determine how close these beliefs are to reality for the students in our school.

## Qualitative Data—Handling Descriptions

For organizing or reducing data of a more qualitative nature, such as student descriptions of instructional strategies, records and descriptions of events such as teacher logs and journals, and document analysis such as which reading comprehension strategies are included in the whole-language basal, the team is dealing primarily with words, not numbers. In an example identified earlier where students and teachers were keeping logs of instructional activities during two five-day periods, and student teachers were serving as observers and recorders in a sample of the classrooms, the team and staff ended up with a stack of data.

There are any number of ways to approach a data-reduction task of this nature, and a thorough description of these options is not possible here. However, I will attempt to provide a few conceptual guidelines and some examples from schools that will enable most teams to use these rich data sources. Again, if any teachers, administrators, or assistants in your school are experienced in conducting qualitative research, use your own in-house experts. As always, reach outside for technical assistance if you feel yourselves becoming buried in a mountain of data, and you do not know how to proceed.

My primary reminder or guideline is to *keep your inquiry mode going*. Treat the responses and documents like a giant inductive set: At the simplest level you are searching for categories and their attributes—figuring out what things go together (convergence). For responses to open-ended survey or interview questions, read through the set quickly for a general impression. Then take each item, and list or group all responses together. Look at this list and decide if there are responses similar in content that appear frequently.

For example, one team interviewed a sample of eighteen students—six from the 6th grade, six from the 7th, and six from the 8th—using four questions. One of the questions asked the students to describe what helped them learn a new task or learn new information. As the team looked at these eighteen responses on the first pass, they noticed immediately that projects of various sorts were mentioned frequently. On the next pass, they looked more closely at the comments students made during their discussion of projects. They noted that students gave descriptions of projects across subject areas, in science, social studies, math, and reading.

As team members continued to distill these responses into information beyond the individual student, they discovered that nine of the ten students who had identified projects as a preferred approach to learning new information or skills had also included work with a partner or small group as part of their description of "doing a project." The team's final description of this most frequently occurring response read, "Projects with a partner or small group." As part of their report to the larger school community, they selected from the interviews several verbatim comments in which students described why projects worked for them. Here is one example: "Like in math, we [my partner and I] read about it, then we make things that show it, we put it all together, and then we talk about it together, and then I know it."

From this set of interviews, the next most common response or category (five students) had to do with the nature of explanations provided by the teacher or by other students. The team went through a process similar to the one described previously to distill a description from across responses. The description read, "Explanations with examples and demonstrations." For this category, there was a subset of three students who emphasized the *willingness* of the teacher to provide additional explanations and the importance of the teacher's not being "mad," "upset," or "treating you like a dummy." In their report to the faculty, the team shared the information from this subset as a separate topic following the information on explanations as the second preferred approach to learning identified by this sample of middle school students.

When working with school teams and faculties on the reduction, display, and analysis of qualitative data, I have frequently been amazed by what we have discovered and what teachers have discovered about how students are experiencing school and about the students' perceptions of instruction, content, and activities. Finding the time to collect and handle the data is the most common concern expressed by school team and faculty members using qualitative data to sharpen their picture of student life relevant to their collective goal. Most groups who have interviewed students have become almost addicted to this method as a way of increasing their understanding of the phenomena under investigation.

## Resources and Other Sources of Assistance _____

As your staff conducts its inquiry, build your professional resource library. Build it both in terms of the content of your collective goal—such as increasing student achievement through cooperative learning and increasing student skill in writing—and in terms of the tools of disciplined inquiry (action research). In the case of qualitative methodology, here are five sources I have found to be most useful:

- *Qualitative Data Analysis: A Sourcebook of New Methods* (Miles and Huberman 1984);
- *Qualitative Evaluation Methods* (Patton 1980);
- *Content Analysis: An Introduction to Its Methodology* (Krippendorf 1980);
- *Ethnography and Qualitative Design in Educational Research* (Goetz and LeCompte 1984); and
- *Qualitative Research for Education* (Bogdan and Biklen 1982).

If you have a staff member who enjoys manipulating data, you are fortunate because this person can coach the team and the staff, serving as an in-house technical assistant. Also, several of your staff may have excellent resource books that will help in organizing data. One I often recommend for quantitative data analysis, beyond those mentioned earlier, is *Statistics: A Spectator Sport* (Jaeger 1983). Also, the chapter on "Data Analysis" in Sagor's (1992) *How to Conduct Collaborative Action Research* provides another example of turning qualitative data into information to inform collective decisions.

Many faculties find they need technical assistance with ways of organizing, displaying, and communicating data on a schoolwide initiative. Sometimes a brief consultation will suffice; sometimes a few phone calls will do it. Often people in the district or the immediate local area can provide the necessary assistance. They can look at data sources and, in 30 minutes, provide models for organization that could take a faculty three months of trial and error and frustration to discover. Why reinvent the wheel if the pattern can be copied and then modified if desired? Seek help and conserve staff time and energy for other purposes—such as analyzing the results.

## Guidelines and Recommendations for Phase 3

Once data have been gathered, they need to be organized expeditiously and shared promptly with the faculty. After a baseline picture has been formed from the data collected and the faculty has determined or reaffirmed its collective goal(s), the use of organized data is for assessing growth or measuring change—not for summation. The mindset of using collective data diagnostically or formatively instead of using the collected results judgmentally or summatively is critical to living the inquiry of action research. Each data-collection cycle and its results should not be thought of as an activity with a grade for the faculty's and students' efforts; it should be thought of as information on the progress being made toward attaining the collective goal and as information to assist all members of the organization as they make decisions for current and future action at the individual, classroom, and school level.

Some highly motivated and concerned faculties collect schoolwide data, but they never "get around to organizing it." Sometimes the raw data from students and teachers are still sitting around months later in dusty manila folders. For myriad reasons—from time management to fear of disrupting cultural norms—no one has transformed the data collected into information to be used. Watch out if time slips by and collected data sit around waiting to be organized. Some faculties and facilitation teams have found it productive, based on their own prior experiences, to schedule set times for data organization into their action plan.

In review, the key technical points to keep in mind as you organize your schoolwide data are:

1. Keep it simple.

2. Disaggregate both quantitative and qualitative data if this process will yield a more clarified picture of what students are experiencing.

3. Schedule time for organization of data.

4. Share the data with the staff as promptly as possible.

5. Seek technical assistance if needed.

By keeping it simple, I mean *count* instances, events, and artifacts; *display* the results in simple tables and charts or brief reports with examples; arrange data so that *meaning is clarified*, not obfuscated; and *organize data by classroom, grade level, and school when appropriate.*

These organized data are the content for the collective study that occurs during the data-analysis phase of schoolwide action research.

# 7
# Phase 4:
# Analyzing and
# Interpreting Data

Data of varying quality are plentiful.
Understanding is rare.
(Alvin Toffler, *Powershift*, 1990, p. 289.)

ESSENTIALLY, DURING THE DATA-ANALYSIS PHASE, THE FACULTY AS A whole and the study groups ask themselves: "What do these data mean?" This phase of the action research process involves turning the data into information to aid the faculty in making decisions. Time needs to be provided for the faculty to study, discuss, and question the data as a professional collective; to determine priority area(s) for action; and to decide what can be celebrated.

When the school staff studies the organized data, what does it say about what's happening to students? This is the time to look at the data that have been collected and ask questions of it and based on it. How many 1st grade boys are failing? How many 3rd graders aren't reading at all outside of class? How many 5th graders don't know their basic math facts, are scoring poorly on math subtests of standardized tests, and dislike math as a subject? How many 7th graders cannot read their content area textbooks and articulate a lack of academic self-esteem in one or more curriculum areas? How many 9th graders dropped out last year, and based on current grades and previous academic histories, how many can be expected to drop out this year? How often are 11th graders writing and at what level?

During this phase of action research, faculty members look at the data they have collected from multiple sources and seek information. Here are some common data-analysis questions:

1. What important points do these data reveal?

2. What patterns or trends show up? Can they be explained?

3. How do data from various sources—test scores, grades, surveys, interviews, observations, and documents—compare or contrast?

4. Do any correlations seem important?

5. Are there results that are different from what you expected?

6. What actions are indicated?

Most data need to be organized and analyzed on at least three levels: school, grade level, and classroom. It is this last level, closest to the action, that creates the most conflict in schoolwide action research. But analysis generally needs to occur at all levels. If not, the school mean can wipe out areas of in-house promise and conceal areas of greatest need—leaving many individual students within the same building experiencing severely inequitable educational opportunities. Although school-level data can indicate there is a problem, they can mask its severity; it is the grade- and class-level data (and for the teacher it is individual student data) that provide the primary diagnostic data needed to guide schoolwide collective action.

## Sharing Data

How these data are shared and analyzed is up to each staff or facilitation team to determine. A few schools have a culture that makes sharing at all three levels easy. Other schools lack such a nurturant culture. Their norms discourage sharing what happens to classroom groups of students; their norms encourage private data analysis. These schools may opt initially to share their classroom data only within their grade-level team or department. But, eventually, as the school becomes a healthier learning community, the results of what students are experiencing on common initiatives should become information for the professional collective body of the school. From such data, we know where we need to focus additional attention and action and what accomplishments we can celebrate.

The faculty, working in study groups and as a total group, sift, sort, and squeeze the data for maximum information. However, they avoid assumptions not warranted by the data—such as looking at the scores on a district-administered, multiple-choice, criterion-referenced test and responding, "This new integrated language arts program we're using in 3rd grade is no better than our old basal program. Our students aren't scoring any better this year in phonics than our last year's students." The inquiry mode and the use of multiple data sources help the faculty avoid rapid conclusions that might not be accurate.

See Chapter 6 (in the discussion of Xandia High School's suspension data, and Figure 6.1) for an example of turning existing data into information for action. An example of turning conventional data into information for the school community is provided from the work of the staff at Sawyer Elementary School in Ames, Iowa.

The schoolwide goal for Sawyer Elementary was to improve the quality of student writing with an emphasis on writing across the curriculum. The data sources included writing samples collected from all students; interviews of all students (What are your favorite kinds of writing? When you write, what helps you get started? What's your favorite way of sharing your writing? etc.); and writing attitude surveys administered to all students (I like to write. / I like writing class stories. / I like to write stories with a partner. / I like to share my writing. / Writing is important. / etc.). After analyzing the results of these initial data sources, each teacher selected three students: one whose writing was at a high level of development within the class; one whose writing was at a medium level; and one whose writing was at a low level of development. Pieces written by these three students were brought to study team meetings throughout the year and analyzed and discussed as teachers sought more information about how students developed as writers and about how instruction influenced this development.

The information shared in Figure 7.1 is a sample of what members of this faculty discovered. Each teacher studied all the information gathered at her grade level and across the grades; each teacher wrote summaries representing what she was learning about students' attitudes and skills in

---

**Figure 7.1**

**Turning Data into Diagnostic Information**

**Grade 1 Teacher**

Of the three children whose writing growth I studied most closely through the action research process, my emerging writer appears to have made the greatest progress from being almost a nonwriter to writing in a logical, enthusiastic fashion. Now, he easily puts his thoughts into writing and feels good about his writing. I feel that his parents' reading to him daily has helped him become a *writer*! The middle student's writing developed more depth; she is able and willing to share more about what she is thinking. My student who was already a fine writer when she entered first grade has shown regular, incremental improvements in the "richness" of details included in her writing; she often incorporates daily activities as examples. She has gradually developed "a sense of piece" in her writing.

All three students have made substantial growth in writing since September. All write easily each day; in fact, they *want* to write daily. They all have an understanding of staying on topic. The most difficult area appears to be developing their pieces in a logical manner.

**Grade 5 Teacher**

My lower-level writer *gained confidence*. His sense of how to put together a story or piece increased along with his elaboration of ideas to support or carry the story. In mechanics, he has expanded his use of sentence structure beyond simple sentences, made some improvements in capitalization and punctuation, while paragraphing remained poor. After much work with the writing process, modeling of the process, and work with buddies, he still does not attend to the details of revision.

My middle-level student became more confident as a writer. She developed greater competence in planning her piece and in planning story line and plots. Her fluency increased, and her voice became clear and distinct. Through practice and instruction, she became more skilled in organizing and sequencing events.

My most skilled writer remained highly motivated and full of ideas. His descriptive skills, artful use of language, and development of plot got better and more skillful. This came primarily from his own attention and diligence. He now sees

(*continued on next page*)

---

**Figure 7.1—*continued***

himself as a writer and continues to write on his own. Instruction that provided an open-ended but focused type of writing to work on really expanded his repertoire of types of writing to try. Without my assignments, he would not have become so versatile a writer, I think.

The matrix helped me target some skills for writing instruction. It will be more beneficial next time around. I feel I didn't do enough writing with my students to develop more progress. But now I have a clearer picture of what to look for with students and what would

---

writing. For example, the information labeled "Grade 1 Teacher" is a synthesis across multiple data sources. At the end of the year, the Sawyer Facilitation Team led the faculty in synthesizing what had been learned about student writing that year. (See "School Summary" in Figure 7.1 for a glimpse of what this faculty learned.) This year, the Sawyer faculty continues its inquiry into improving the communication skills of its students and into using writing as an aid to problem solving in mathematics.

### Guidelines and Recommendations for Phase 4

During each data-analysis phase, we transform all the "stuff" collected into information that helps us assess the current status of our schoolwide goal. The faculty as a unit and in study groups question the data as a professional collective and squeeze the data for maximum information. We take this useful information and determine priority area(s) for action and decide what can be celebrated.

Once results are found that are not acceptable in a healthy learning environment, then the questions of "Why?" and "What can we do to change these results?" arise. These questions lead the faculty to another level of data analysis. Now, we study the data and reflect on what students experience in our school—seeking possible causes or reasons for poor performance and guidance toward actions that might improve student performance in our area of interest.

## Prior to Phase 5: Studying the Professional Literature

So far in this chapter, we have concentrated on the use of on-site data. Now, we move beyond our internal sources to those external to our school site. As we study the professional literature, we seek information from across and beyond our profession. We gather and study information from our present colleagues and from powerful sources left to us by earlier scholars. Remember our funnel, with on-site data from our school and with data from other schools, districts, and the literature being "poured" into the collective decision-making process of the faculty.

Either simultaneous with Phases 1–4 or following Phase 4, *we inquire into the literature.* We study these external sources with processes similar to those we applied to our on-site data:

1. Identify topics in the literature that relate to the area of interest and would be most likely to yield useful information for the staff.

2. Gather or collect research reports, research syntheses, articles, books, and videotapes in these areas.

3. Organize these materials for study.

4. Analyze and interpret the information they provide for understanding the collective area of interest and for generating possible actions to be taken.

5. Determine the most promising actions schools can employ for improving student lives.

The facilitation team or a task force needs to take responsibility for gathering a base of research reports, articles, and other resources and for sifting through these items for the most appropriate documents and media for use by the total faculty. In selecting this subset of sources for study, the team's criteria for inclusion are the match to the area of interest or the collective goal if identified, the quality of the research articles, and the conceptual rigor of the thought pieces. What is critical to the success of this collective study of the literature is that these sources be of the highest quality possible—worthy of dozens of professionals giving hours of their lives distilling meaning from them.

### Using Research Articles and Meta-Analyses

For school faculties aiming directly at improving student learning, excellent research syntheses and meta-analyses are available. For example:

Bloom (1984). "The 2 Sigma Problem: The Search for Group Instruction as Effective as One-to-One Tutoring."

Bredderman (1983). "Effects of Activity-Based Elementary Science on Student Outcomes: A Quantitative Synthesis."

Dole, Duffy, Roehler, and Pearson (1991). "Moving from the Old to the New: Research on Reading Comprehension Instruction."

Englert, Raphael, Anderson, Anthony, and Stevens (1991). "Making Strategies and Self-Talk Visible: Writing Instruction in Regular and Special Education Classes."

Hillocks (1987). "Synthesis of Research on Teaching Writing."

Madden, Slavin, Karweit, Dolan, and Wasik (1993). "Success for All: Longitudinal Effects of a Restructuring Program for Inner-City Elementary Schools."

Slavin and Madden (1989). "What Works for Students at Risk: A Research Synthesis."

Everyone on staff will have access to the base set gathered by the team, but items selected for more intense analysis will be the content of study-group and faculty meetings. When study groups are not planning lessons or discussing and analyzing their on-site data or their teaching strategies, they are sifting and squeezing the best resources available in our common literature. [See Chapter 8 on surveying curricular and instructional initiatives in *The Self-Renewing School* (Joyce, Wolf, and Calhoun 1993).]

I have found that structured-response sheets are useful in helping groups with cooperative processing of these external resources. (See Figure 7.2 and Appendix Item 5).

Often, there are groans from the faculty when I mention this aspect of schoolwide action research. These groans occur for various reasons—ranging from the technical language of the reports, to the lack of time for reading, to the chore of making inferences from the reports that are appropriate to the school site, to a general resistance to external information, to an articulated belief that "our school is so unique that nothing in these articles applies to our needs." I know of no easy way to help the culture of the school become one where serious study of our craft, including what others have learned or thought, is a normal part of professionals working together. My best advice on this is the same I offered on getting started with action research: "Just do it until it becomes normative."

---

**Figure 7.2**

**Structured Response Sheet for Articles or Videotapes**

Title of Article or Videotape _____

Author or Presenter _____

1. What does this author say to us about content? (For example, if the collective goal aims at improving student achievement in mathematics: What knowledge, skills, and processes of mathematics need to be part of the daily/yearly curriculum?)

2. What does this author say to us about instruction? (Continuing with the mathematics example: What recommendations are made or can be inferred about the presentation of content or the design of instruction to enhance students' understanding and use of mathematics?)

3. What does this author say to us about assessing student learning? (Continuing with mathematics: Are there suggestions about how to diagnose students' knowledge, skill, or use of mathematics?)

---

## Guidelines and Recommendations for Studying the Professional Literature

The same inquiry mode is used in exploring the literature as is used in studying on-site data about what students are experiencing. Simply, we seek external sources of information to combine with our internal sources as we make decisions for collective action. *Informed decision making is what action research is all about.*

The facilitation team and faculty select the best articles and resources available; study-group members discuss and analyze these resources for usefulness to their area(s) of interest. These resources may provide ideas for innovations in instruction, curriculum, and assessment or for changes in how students, materials, resources, and staff are administered or managed. As the faculty learns how to study together, structured-response sheets and cooperative processing activities are useful in building collective knowledge.

Mann (personal communication 1989) states, "America is redesigning its education system. And as usual, we are doing it as the haphazard result of thousands of unrelated decisions and trends." Collective, disciplined inquiry into what other educators have learned can help us avoid this fragmentation and avoid some of the pendulum swings from one fad to the next. In schoolwide action research, we use our professional literature to identify and develop innovations and to generate initiatives that will improve student learning: *we use our professional literature to support school renewal.*

# 8
# Phase 5: Taking Action

THE KEY QUESTIONS THAT GUIDE THE ACTION RESEARCH PROCESS
in Phase 5 are: Should we act differently? If yes, how?
The information provided through the analysis and
interpretation of on-site data and the analysis
and interpretation of the professional literature focus
collective action on those options most likely to yield
positive benefits for students.

Analyses of data and their implications for collective
action serve as powerful "choice points" for a school staff,
as both "noticing choice" and "doing choice." Paraphrasing
Weick on the role of choice in the organizing process, the
staff asks itself: "Knowing what we know now, should we
*notice* something we did not notice before and ignore
something we noticed before?" and "Knowing what we know
now, should we act differently?" From the initial collection
of baseline data to the regular checks on progress
performed during data analyses, the staff faces a series of
choice points for unfreezing action and changing the
experience of schooling for its students. Phase 5 is a major
choice point for unfreezing action.

During Phase 5, we combine and apply what we are
learning from studying our on-site data and the professional
literature. *We use the knowledge gained from these collective
studies to select innovations and develop initiatives that have
the best chance of improving student learning.*

The actions/innovations selected by your faculty will
depend on the content of the common goal and the findings
from their study of the professional literature. *Now is the
time for the faculty to select a few—one to three—innovative
strategies and maybe a few administrative changes to
implement schoolwide. The innovations selected need to*

> *focus primarily on instruction and curriculum. The administrative/managerial changes need to be integrative and lead to the improved health of the organization (both its clients, the students; and its members, the staff), with no punitive side effects for students or teachers.* Here are some examples of actions that often have punitive side effects for students: stricter discipline codes that lead to greater absence from instruction; higher academic standards without accompanying changes in instruction; and adding another "track" that leads to increased segregation of the student population.

## Selecting Innovations and Developing Initiatives That Focus on Student Learning

> What teachers do in the structuring of learning opportunities and the provision of instruction is at the heart of the contribution schools make to the academic achievement of students.
> (Hawley, Rosenholtz, Goodstein, and Hasselbring, *Peabody Journal of Education*, 1984)

Schools exist partially because society believes that teaching works. Yet, it is difficult for many faculties to focus on schoolwide improvement of teaching. One irony in this dilemma is that teaching or instruction is an area over which faculties have the most control. We cannot change the home environment of our students; we cannot change the parents of our students; we cannot exchange the student population we have in attendance for a new student population. In some cases, we cannot change the adopted curriculum materials. However, we can rapidly change the instruction our students experience.

And, there is always an *up*. No matter how good and effective we are as teachers or how high the standardized test scores are for our school, there is room for growth. From Thomas Edison to Albert Einstein to Joe Montana to good teachers and administrators across the world, the improvement of ideas, skills, craft, and contributions were and are always possible. It's a bit like the saying "Grow or die" or, more positively phrased, "Lifelong learning as part of professional life."

We know that collective inquiry focused on student learning is tough work for schools. Faculties sometimes take one to three years in planning without reaching a point of collective action for improving instruction. Why is it so difficult to effect changes in the education offered in classrooms across the school? We have evidence from Goodlad (1984), from Sirotnik (1987), from Strusinski (1989), from Taylor and Teddlie (1992), and from Muncey and McQuillan's (1993) five-year study of the Coalition of Essential Schools that changing the teaching-learning interaction is uncommon and difficult work. Many other studies provide testimonials to this difficulty. David and Peterson's (1984) study of thirty-two elementary schools—located in eight states and identified as exemplary for their success in generating school improvement through shared decision-making—found only a few schools implementing instructional changes. The authors hypothesized that any action that infringed on "teacher autonomy" in the classroom was likely to be avoided, with the majority of these schools focusing their schoolwide collective action on student discipline codes and other noninstructional areas. This was true even among those programs that had been in place for several years.

Overall results of the California School Improvement Program (Berman and Gjelten 1983) were similar—even in this well-funded, long-term, school-based improvement initiative, few schools engaged in instructional change around a collectively valued goal. Rosenholtz (1989) found most schools "stuck" or "almost stuck," with little ability to implement or maintain major instructional innovations. Results of Louis and Miles' national survey of 178 urban high schools that were implementing comprehensive improvement programs and that were showing signs of progress indicate that very few schools were engaging in instructional improvement. A quote from *Improving the Urban High School* (Louis and Miles 1990) sharply illustrates the depth of the problem:

> Programs implemented for less than three years show significantly less impact on student achievement, student attendance, teaching methods, new teacher skills, and student-faculty relations than those that have been in place longer. [Even] if we look only at those programs that have

been implemented for three or more years, the conclusion that effective schools programs have greater impact on the cosmetic and administrative side of schools than on the teaching-learning process and student achievement is almost inescapable (p. 49).

The results of the case studies of five urban high schools designated as "especially promising" in terms of improvement support this same pattern of reluctance to engage in instructional change (Louis and Miles 1990). In two of these five cases, the comprehensive school improvement plans did not affect "what went on 'behind the classroom door,' but focused more on improving the safety of the school, ensuring that students were actually in attendance, and increasing attention to surface climate issues" (pp. 41–42). Reviewing the fifty-one improvement themes identified in the five schools over the course of the study indicates that only six themes appear to be directly related to instruction.

*Let's acknowledge that school renewal is tough work. But let's also acknowledge that with shared decision making, collective study, and more informed decisions that lead to concerted action, most faculties can create learning environments for their students and for themselves that are far beyond the present reality.*

Just by conducting action research, faculties begin to address problems. They have chosen to notice something. Exploit the benefits of this attention factor and use these benefits to increase organizational efficacy. Some faculties, when confronted with the severity of the problem and its effects on students' lives, have taken action during the data-collection phase. For example, faculty members at one school were shocked when they counted the number of children in their learning community who were failing the 9th grade and the number who had traditionally dropped out; and the faculty took immediate action that ranged from instituting cross-grade partners to a community/business campaign to reduce school absences. Other more complex activities, such as cooperative learning across departments, were instituted as the faculty members moved through the action research process—but they felt morally compelled to act immediately because of the implications of their initial data collection.

A few of the actions taken by this high school in Phase 5 include:

- reorganizing its 8th grade orientation to include current students, parent representatives, and extracurricular representatives at the on-site orientation and to include students, counselors, and an administrator at orientations held at each feeder middle school;
- reorganizing new student orientation;
- creating a videotape for the middle school exploratory course;
- having 9th–12th graders write letters to be used in the exploratory course;
- offering a four-week/half-day intensive basic skills course in reading and mathematics for over-age 8th graders/rising 9th graders whose academic histories indicated they were at immediate risk for dropping out if they entered high school without prior intervention; and
- implementing cooperative learning across classrooms, supported by staff development.

Go for innovations that are most likely to improve learning for all students; make administrative/managerial changes that support the evolution of an integrative learning community. Initiate innovations such as cooperative learning across subject areas, the inquiry approach across subject areas, integrating the language arts, and global literacy; make administrative changes such as cross-grade grouping, tutoring programs, computers assigned to student work teams, and basic skills immersion courses for the summer taught by teachers, students, and parents. *These innovations and managerial changes become the schoolwide initiative for collective implementation.*

## Developing or Modifying Action Plans

Now is the time to craft both short- and long-term action plans. Here is where our traditional planning-process skills are most useful. We know how to design action plans that indicate specific tasks to be accomplished, who will be responsible, what materials or assistance is needed, how success will be measured, and when tasks will be accomplished. We have lived this process in developing hundreds of classroom lesson plans, in completing group projects in university courses, and in developing comprehensive plans for our school or for an area of central-office interest.

The action plan developed as part of Phase 5 pulls together what the faculty has learned and describes how it will be applied. At the most basic level, the faculty develops a "living plan" for concerted action. Through this plan, those innovations and administrative or managerial changes that the faculty deems most promising are woven together into a public schoolwide initiative. The action plan publishes this initiative, which represents the best decisions of the faculty at this point in time and publicizes its continuing commitment to assess the effects of these decisions. Simply put, *the action plan specifies how the collective inquiry into improved student learning will proceed.*

Let's take a moment to distinguish between innovations and initiatives. Innovations are actions that faculty members identify—or create—from their experience and their study of the professional literature. Initiatives are the "living plans" that faculty members design to implement the innovations and changes they have decided to pursue through concerted, collective action. The schoolwide initiative is published through the action plan.

The same data sources used in Phases 2–4 or a combination of new and old sources can form part of the new action plan and be used to assess the effects of the actions selected by the faculty. So the action research cycle repeats with the same learning goal and with actions being implemented that will help the school attain this goal. *The tricky thing at this point is that now there are two lines of assessment occurring: one, to determine progress in student learning; two, to determine the implementation status of the selected innovations and changes.*

Therefore, action plans need to include techniques for studying implementation. These techniques can be as simple as teacher logs of numbers of times per week teachers use a particular instructional strategy; records of number of minutes per day teachers provide instruction on mathematical word problems using manipulables; lists of science concepts being taught weekly and the strategies used; school matrixes with each cell depicting total number of student compositions, mean, and numerical range of compositions in each classroom (see Figure 8.1 for an example). Action plans may also include more sophisticated studies of implementation, such as a combination of observations, teacher logs, and student logs, or a peer-coaching approach if the innovation'(s) require a change in classroom instruction.

In summary, an action plan describes the schoolwide initiative that will be implemented and assessed by the faculty. This written "living plan" includes these elements: what, who, when, which resources, and how progress will be assessed. Both the effects on student learning and the implementation of selected actions are assessed. Faculty members look at data from both sources as they determine progress and make decisions for further action.

## Moving Into Action

Phase 5 is a critical time for building organizational efficacy. Thus far, two primary times are critical points at which school teams are most likely to delay action that would affect students and instruction: before initial data collection (Phase 2) and during the identification of schoolwide actions to be taken (part of Phase 5; the other part is implementation). Especially at these times, actions are delayed as leadership teams or faculties opt for more planning time or for more time to build staff readiness. Planning, though essential, must not function as a barrier to change. Cultural readiness for change, although optimal to have in advance, can be developed by engaging successfully in collective action—an old-fashioned, educational, Deweyan "learning by doing" approach.

If possible, take some kind of action immediately and closely watch its effects on students. A staff that accomplishes something early begins to build collective confidence that can support more difficult changes. Regrettably, most schools must work to build a sense of collective efficacy. Here is a simple example of immediate action: A staff interested in improving student behavior or interested in cooperative learning to increase listening comprehension and social cohesion, can—without any additional planning, materials, or technical or staff development assistance—just ask students to confer in

**Figure 8.1**
**Crawford Elementary School Action Plan Worksheet**
**October 1993**

*Goal: To improve student expository writing.*

| Tasks | Target Date | Responsibility | Resources |
|---|---|---|---|
| 1. Develop action plan Study the critical attributes of expository writing. | Sept.-Oct. | All staff members (Study Teams) | Research articles—textbooks—Language Arts resource books Meet with Nina—Marilyn—Marcia Meet with Sawyer Staff—Edwards Staff |
| 2. Develop/adopt analytical scale for evaluation | Oct.-Nov. | All staff members | Meet with Tony—Marilyn—Nina Look at scales that have already been developed Look at matrix from Sawyer |
| 3. Collect baseline writing samples and determine data-collection process: formal or informal, frequency, which students | Oct. | K–6 classroom teachers All staff members | Tony VanderZyl's work with staff on analysis |
| 4. Determine specific areas to improve | Nov. | Study teams study student writing samples and identify target areas for improvement | |
| 5. Investigate instructional strategies; develop classroom action plans | Nov. | Study teams | Group Language Experience Strategy Inductive Lessons on the Reading/Writing Connection |

*(continued on next page)*

| | | | |
|---|---|---|---|
| 6. Implement plans | Dec.-May | Individual teachers with the support of their study team | |
| 7. Collect and analyze writing samples and share results; conference with students | Dec.-May | Same | |
| 8. Modify actions based on results | Dec.-May | Same | Share and develop lessons together |
| 9. Repeat #7 and #8 often | Dec.-May | Same | |
| 10. Final data collection, analysis, and report to the district | April-May | All staff Building Leadership Team | |
| 11. Celebrate improvement in student expository writing | Ongoing & May | All staff and students | |
| 12 Use information to create new goal and plan | May | All staff | |

*Note:* Shared with permission of Crawford Elementary School, Ames, Iowa.

pairs over content and generate questions. Most of us could do this for a few minutes several times a day or once per class period and record changes in classroom instructional climate.

Here is an example of long-term action. A faculty or district decides to focus on developing the literate world citizen. Their immediate focus is to improve student skills in and attitudes toward reading and writing as methods of communication. They study student outcome data, such as disaggregated standardized test results, grade distributions, and courses taken; gather data on the quantity and quality of student writing and reading; and study the professional literature. They decide that their curriculum area for several years of intensive collective study will be language arts. They decide to use an integrated approach to teaching language arts with a heavy emphasis on children's literature, the reading-writing connection, and the inductive approaches to teaching. They study the effects of these decisions through repeated cycles of schoolwide action research, modifying and deleting actions as indicated by the data and by their collective experience in learning to implement these complex innovations. (Thanks to my colleagues in Ames Community Schools for living this example of schoolwide and districtwide action research.)

*The "temporary" culminating activity of Phase 5 is implementing our selected actions.* Lewin reminded us in the '40s that it takes research, action, and training for individuals to identify problems and achieve organizational goals. As major instructional innovations are selected by the faculty for implementation, quality staff development will be needed to assist the staff in adding these strategies or approaches to their teaching repertoire.

Resource people to assist with this staff development may be available in your school, at your county office, at another school in a district nearby, in the regional service agency, or at the local university. Excellent written resources include articles such as "Cooperative Learning and Staff Development: Teaching the Method with the Method" (Joyce 1992) and books such as *Student Achievement through Staff Development* (Joyce and Showers 1995). What is obvious today is that one- and two-day workshops, or even five-day workshops without follow-up and without the collegial support provided by study groups, will not support the implementation of curriculum or instructional innovations. As you move into implementing your selected actions, set yourselves up for success. (See Appendix Item 6.) Be sure to include training and follow-up support in your action plan.

## Guidelines and Recommendations for Phase 5

Phase 5 answers the question, "What do we do?" While the faculty may take action during other phases of the process, it is during Phase 5 that the facilitation team and the faculty design the primary initiative to which collective energy will be channeled. They select and create innovations, fashion then into a collective initiative focused on student learning, and move into action as individuals and as an organization.

They juxtapose on-site information about students with information available in the professional literature, especially research reports (both qualitative and quantitative). Then the facilitation team and faculty combine the innovations and administrative changes they have selected into a schoolwide initiative. This initiative, and the innovations and changes that compose it, is the means to an end. Its primary purpose is to enhance student learning as identified by the collective goal; its secondary purpose is to enhance the learning of all members of the organization.

The written action plan publishes the schoolwide initiative and describes the procedures of this collective inquiry. As faculty members begin to implement the actions specified in the plan, Phase 2 and the collection of data begin again.

When does action research stop? . . . When the faculty is satisfied, when it has no more questions to answer, when it has no more problems to solve. Until then, the cycles of action research continue, with all members of the faculty studying data relevant to student learning, studying data on the implementation of selected changes, using the professional literature, and taking action until they are content with the results.

# A Closing Note

The quest for school renewal through action research . . .

- is a route to immediate student outcomes;
- can develop the school as a learning community;
- can build organizational capacity to solve problems;
- is a staff development program through the study of literature and on-site data and the determination of optimum actions for implementation; and
- can be personal and professional development.

To integrate action research into the culture of a school as a normal mode of operation, we must foster and continuously tend social efficacy and ensure technical support throughout the move from innovation to permanent practice. As we experiment with and implement action research, we build our learning community. We actualize our belief in the efficacy of schools and of ourselves as professionals: We can learn to conduct action research, to support it in practice, and to make it a natural part of our organizational life.

Part of the promise inherent in action research is its use as a model to support the current movement toward "site-based" decision making. That movement is designed to improve curriculum and instruction, leading to greater student learning and greater equity of educational opportunity. Schoolwide action research provides some structure for collective inquiry and "site-based" renewal. We gather information about our students, from each other, and from people and resources beyond our school site; and we use this combination of information to improve the education of all students entrusted to us.

Here is my final reminder on conducting schoolwide action research: *Make your action research process a fun and productive experience.* Learn, and enjoy the learning and collegiality of professionals working together and helping students grow.

# Bibliography

Allen, J., J. Combs, M. Hendricks, P. Nash, and S. Wilson. (1988). "Studying Change: Teachers Who Became Researchers." *Language Arts* 65, 4: 379–387.

Bennis, W.G. (1989). *Why Leaders Can't Lead*. San Francisco: Jossey-Bass.

Berman, P., and T. Gjelten. (1983). *Improving School Improvement*. Berkeley, Calif.: Berman, Weiler Associates.

Bloom, B.S. (1984). "The 2 Sigma Problem: The Search for Group Instruction as Effective as One-to-One Tutoring." *Educational Researcher* 13, 3: 4–16.

Bogdan, R.C., and S.K. Biklen. (1982). *Qualitative Research in Education*. Boston: Allyn and Bacon.

Bredderman, T. (1983). "Effects of Activity-Based Elementary Science on Student Outcomes: A Quantitative Synthesis." *Review of Educational Research* 53, 4: 499–518.

Bruner, J.S. (1973). *The Relevance of Education*. New York: Norton.

Calhoun, E.F. (1991). "A Wide-Angle Lens: How to Increase the Variety, Collection, and Use of Data for School Improvement." In *Lessons from the Field: Renewing Schools Through Shared Governance and Action Research*, edited by C.D. Glickman and L. Allen. Athens: Program for School Improvement, College of Education, University of Georgia.

Calhoun, E.F. (1992). "A Status Report on Action Research in the League of Professional Schools." In *Lessons from the League: Improving Schools through Shared Governance and Action Research*, Vol. 2, edited by C.D. Glickman and L. Allen. Athens: Program for School Improvement, College of Education, University of Georgia.

Calhoun, E.F. (1993). "Action Research: Three Approaches." *Educational Leadership* 51, 2: 62–65.

Calhoun, E.F., and C.D. Glickman. (1993). "Issues and Dilemmas of Action Research in the League of Professional Schools." Paper presented at the annual meeting of the American Educational Research Association, Atlanta.

Carr, W., and S. Kemmis. (1983). *Becoming Critical: Knowing Through Action Research*. Geelong, Victoria: Deakin Press.

Carkhuff, R.R. (1973). *The Art of Problem-Solving*. Amherst, Mass.: Human Resource Development Press.

Casley, D.J., and K. Kumar. (1988). *The Collection, Analysis, and Use of Monitoring and Evaluation Data*. Published for the World Bank. Baltimore: Johns Hopkins Press.

Chein, I., S.W. Cook, and J. Harding. (1948). "The Field of Action Research." *The American Psychologist* 3, 2: 43–50.

Corey, S.M. (1949). "Curriculum Development Through Action Research." *Educational Leadership* 7, 3: 147–153.

Corey, S.M. (1953). *Action Research to Improve School Practices*. New York: Teachers College Press.

Crandall, D., S. Loucks, M. Huberman, and M. Miles. (1982). *People, Policies, and Practices: Examining the Chain of School Improvement*. Vols. I–X. Andover, Mass.: The Network.

David, J.L. (1990). "Restructuring: Increased Autonomy and Changing Roles." Invited address presented at the annual meeting of the American Educational Research Association, Boston.

David, J.L., and S. M. Peterson. (1984). "Can Schools Improve Themselves? A Study of School-Based Improvement Programs." Palo Alto, Calif.: Bay Area Research Group.

Dewey, J. (1910). *How We Think*. Boston: Heath.

Dewey, J. (1904/1965). "The Relationship of Theory to Practice in Education." In *Teacher Education in America: A Documentary History*, edited by M.L. Borrowman. New York: Teachers College Press.

Dicker, M. (1990). "Using Action Research to Navigate an Unfamiliar Teaching Assignment." *Theory Into Practice* 29, 3: 203–208.

Dole, J.A., G.G. Duffy, L.H. Roehler, and P.D. Pearson. (1991). "Moving from the Old to the New: Research on Reading Comprehension Instruction." *Review of Educational Research* 61, 2: 239–264.

Englert, C.S., T.E. Raphael, L.M. Anderson, H.M. Anthony, and D.D. Stevens. (1991). "Making Strategies and Self-Talk Visible: Writing Instruction in Regular and Special Education Classes." *American Educational Research Journal* 28, 2: 337–372.

Fullan, M.G., and M.B. Miles. (1992). "Getting Reform Right: What Works and What Doesn't." *Phi Delta Kappan* 73, 10: 744–52.

Fullan, M.G., and A. Pomfret. (1977). "Research on Curriculum and Instruction Implementation." *Review of Educational Research* 47,1: 335–397.

Fullan, M.G., and S. Steigelbauer. (1991). *The New Meaning of Educational Change*. New York: Teachers College Press.

Fuller, F. (1969). "Concerns of Teachers: A Developmental Conceptualization." *American Educational Research Journal* 6, 2: 207–226.

Gardner, J.W. (1963). *Self Renewal: The Individual and the Innovative Society*. New York: Harper and Row

Gardner, J.W. (Winter 1987). "Self Renewal." *National Forum* 67, 1: 16–19.

Glasser, W. (1990). *The Quality School.* New York: HarperPerennial.

Glickman, C.D. (1990). *Supervision of Instruction: A Developmental Approach.* Boston: Allyn and Bacon.

Glickman, C.D. (1993). *Renewing America's Schools: A Guide for School-Based Action.* San Francisco: Jossey-Bass.

Glickman, C.D., and L. Allen, eds. (1991). *Lessons from the Field: Renewing Schools through Shared Governance and Action Research.* Athens: Program for School Improvement, University of Georgia.

Glickman, C.D., and L. Allen, eds. (1992). *Lessons from the League: Improving Schools through Shared Governance and Action Research.* Vol. 2. Athens: Program for School Improvement, University of Georgia.

Glickman, C.D., L. Allen, and B. Lunsford. (1992). "Facilitation of Internal Change: The League of Professional Schools." Paper presented at the annual meeting of the American Educational Research Association, San Francisco.

Goetz, J.P., and M.D. LeCompte. (1984). *Ethnography and Qualitative Design in Educational Research.* Orlando, Fla.: Academic Press.

Goodlad, J.I. (1984). *A Place Called School.* New York: McGraw-Hill.

Hall, G.E., and S.M. Hord. (1987). *Change in Schools: Facilitating the Process.* New York: State University of New York.

Hawley, W.D., S. Rosenholtz, H.J. Goodstein, and T. Hasselbring. (1984). "Good Schools: What Research Says About Improving Student Achievement." Theme issue. *Peabody Journal of Education* 61, 4: 1–178.

Hensley, F., E.F. Calhoun, and C.D. Glickman. (1992). "Results from Site-Based, Action Research Schools: What Has Been Accomplished? What Are the Next Steps?" Paper presented at the annual meeting of the American Educational Research Association, San Francisco.

Hillocks, G. (1987). "Synthesis of Research on Teaching Writing." *Educational Leadership* 44, 8: 71–82.

Holly, P. (1991). "Action Research Within Institutional Development: It's Becoming Second Nature to Us Now." Paper presented at the annual meeting of the American Educational Research Association, Chicago.

Holly, P. (1992). Comments made during an Action Research Workshop. Ames, IA.

Hopkins, D. (1985). *A Teacher's Guide to Classroom Research.* Philadelphia: Open University Press.

Houle, C.O. (1980). *Continuing Learning in the Professions.* San Francisco: Jossey-Bass.

Huberman, A.M. (1992). "Successful School Improvement: Reflections and Observations" (Critical introduction). In *Successful School Improvement,* by M.G. Fullan. London: Open University Press.

Huberman, A.M., and M.B. Miles. (1984). *Innovation Up Close: How School Improvement Works*. New York: Plenum Press.

Huberman, A.M., and M.B. Miles. (1986). "Rethinking the Quest for School Improvement: Some Findings from the DESSI Study." In *Rethinking School Improvement: Research, Craft, and Concept*, edited by A. Lieberman. New York: Teachers College Press.

Hughes, R.G. (1982). "Results of a Survey in 10 South Georgia Counties: Why Classroom Teachers and Administrators Do Not Use More Research Findings in the Classroom and Office." Paper presented at the seventh annual meeting of the Georgia Educational Research Association, Atlanta.

Jaeger, R. (1983). *Statistics: A Spectator Sport*. Beverly Hills: Sage Publications.

Joyce, B.R. (1991). "Doors to School Improvement." *Educational Leadership* 48, 8: 59–62.

Joyce, B.R. (1992). "Cooperative Learning and Staff Development: Teaching the Method with the Method." *Cooperative Learning* 12, 2: 10–13.

Joyce, B., and B. Showers. (1995). *Student Achievement Through Staff Development*. 2nd ed. White Plains, N.Y.: Longman.

Joyce, B., J. Wolf, and E. Calhoun. (1993). *The Self-Renewing School*. Alexandria, Va.: ASCD.

Krippendorf, K. (1980). *Content Analysis: An Introduction to Its Methodology*. Beverly Hills, Calif.: Sage Publications.

Lewin, K. (1946). "Action Research and Minority Problems." In *Resolving Social Conflicts: Selected Papers on Group Dynamics*, by K. Lewin (compiled in 1948). New York: Harper and Row.

Lewin, K. (1947). "Group Decisions and Social Change." In *Readings in Social Psychology*, edited by T.M. Newcomb and E.L. Hartley. New York: Henry Holt.

Lewin, K. (1948). *Resolving Social Conflicts: Selected Papers on Group Dynamics*. New York: Harper and Row.

Lieberman, A., ed. (1988). *Building a Professional Culture in Schools*. New York: Teachers College Press.

Lippitt, G.L., P. Langseth, and J. Mossop. (1985). *Implementing Organizational Change*. San Francisco: Jossey-Bass.

Little, J.W. (1990). "The Persistence of Privacy: Autonomy and Initiative in Teachers' Professional Relations." *Teachers College Record* 91, 4: 509–536.

Louis, K.S., and M.B. Miles. (1990). *Improving the Urban High School*. New York: Teachers College Press.

Madden, N.A., R.E. Slavin, N.L. Karweit, L. Dolan, and B.A. Wasik. (1993). "Success for All: Longitudinal Effects of a Restructuring Program for Inner-City Elementary Schools." *American Educational Research Journal* 30, 1: 123–148.

Marick, R. (1990). "Seattle Portable Writing Project." *Teacher Leadership. Vol. 3. New Skills—New Opportunities*. Seattle: University of Washington, Puget Sound Educational Consortium.

Miles, M.B. (1992). "40 Years of Change in Schools: Some Personal Reflections." Paper presented at the annual meeting of the American Educational Research Association, San Francisco.

Miles, M.B., and A.M. Huberman. (1984). *Qualitative Data Analysis: A Sourcebook of New Methods*. Beverly Hills, Calif.: Sage.

Muncey, D.E., and P.J. McQuillan. (1993). "Preliminary Findings from a Five-Year Study of the Coalition of Essential Schools." *Phi Delta Kappan* 74, 6: 486–489.

Myers, M. (1985). *The Teacher-Researcher: How to Study Writing in the Classroom*. Urbana, Ill.: National Council of Teachers of English.

Oja, S.N., and L. Smulyan. (1989). *Collaborative Action Research: A Developmental Approach*. London: Falmer Press.

Patton, M.Q. (1980). *Qualitative Evaluation Methods*. Beverly Hills, Calif.: Sage.

Reys, R.E., and T. Yeager. (1974). "Elementary Teachers and Research in Mathematics Education." *School Science and Mathematics* 74: 431–436.

Rogers, D., R. Haven-O'Donnell, S. Hebdon, and F. Ferrell. (1990). "Lessons on Relating Research, Reflection, and Reform from Three Researcher/Practitioner Projects." Paper presented at the annual meeting of the American Educational Research Association, Boston.

Rosenholtz, S.J. (1989). *Teachers' Workplace: The Social Organization of Schools*. White Plains, N.Y.: Longman.

Sagor, R. (1991). "What Project LEARN Reveals about Collaborative Action Research." *Educational Leadership* 48, 6: 6–10.

Sagor, R. (1992). *How to Conduct Collaborative Action Research*. Alexandria, Va.: ASCD.

Sarason, S. (1982). *The Culture of the School and the Problem of Change*. 2nd ed. Boston: Allyn and Bacon.

Sarason, S. (1990). *The Predictable Failure of School Reform: Can We Change the Course Before It's Too Late?* San Francisco: Jossey-Bass.

Schaefer, R.J. (1967). *The School as a Center of Inquiry*. New York: Harper and Row.

Schön, D.A. (1987). *Educating the Reflective Practitioner*. San Francisco: Jossey-Bass.

Sirotnik, K.A. (1987). "Evaluation in the Ecology of Schooling." In *The Ecology of School Renewal: The Eighty-Sixth Yearbook of the National Society for the Study of Education*, edited by J.I. Goodlad. Chicago: The University of Chicago Press.

Sizer, T.R. (1991). "No Pain, No Gain." *Educational Leadership* 48, 8: 32–34.

Slavin, R.E., and N.A. Madden. (1989). "What Works for Students at Risk: A Research Synthesis." *Educational Leadership* 46, 5: 4–13.

Sparks, D. (1993). "Insights on School Improvement: An Interview with Larry Lezotte." *Journal of Staff Development* 14, 3: 18–21.

Strickland, D.S. (1988). "The Teacher as Researcher: Toward the Extended Professional." *Language Arts* 65, 8: 754–764.

Strusinski, M. (1989). "The Provision of Technical Support for School-Based Evaluations: The Researcher's Perspective." Paper presented at the annual meeting of the American Educational Research Association, San Francisco.

Sudman, S., and N.M. Bradburn. (1982). *Asking Questions: A Practical Guide to Questionnaire Design.* San Francisco: Jossey-Bass.

Taylor, D.L., and C. Teddlie. (1992). "Restructuring and the Classroom: A View from a Reform District." Paper presented at the annual meeting of the American Educational Research Association, San Francisco.

Thelen, H. (1954). *Dynamics of Groups at Work.* Chicago: University of Chicago Press.

Thelen, H. (1960). *Education and the Human Quest.* New York: Harper and Row.

Tikunoff, W.J., and J.R. Mergendoller. (1983). "Inquiry as a Means to Professional Growth: The Teacher as Researcher." In *Staff Development: Eighty-Second Yearbook of the National Society for the Study of Education*, edited by G.A. Griffin. Chicago: The University of Chicago Press.

Toffler, A. (1990). *Powershift.* New York: Bantam Books.

Weick, K.E. (1969). *The Social Psychology of Organizing.* Reading, Mass: Addison-Wesley.

Whitford, B.L., P.C. Schlecty, and L.G. Shelor. (1987). "Sustaining Action Research Through Collaboration: Inquiries for Invention." *Peabody Journal of Education* 64, 3: 151–169.

# Appendix

## ITEM 1

### Shared-Governance Policy for Thunderbolt Elementary School Chatham County Schools

**Objectives**

1. To provide an ongoing means for initiating and supporting schoolwide improvement.

2. To provide systematic opportunities for staff and administration to develop consensus.

3. To move toward consensus among faculty and administration.

4. To promote a sense of ownership of organizational goals among staff.

5. To provide formal procedures for gathering valid information for problem-identification, decision-making, and problem-solving activities.

6. To increase the level of harmony between individual and staff goals.

**Statement of Purpose**

The governing board is the Executive Council. The purpose of the Executive Council is to:

1. Provide for shared decision making between faculty and administration relating to schoolwide improvement.

2. Provide for a free flow of communication between and among faculty and administration.

3. Provide for improved learning opportunities for students.

---

*Note:* Adopted January 17, 1992. Shared by permission of Thunderbolt Elementary School, Chatham County Schools, Savannah, Georgia.

### Names and Responsibilities of Groups

*The Thunderbolt Elementary School Executive Council for School Improvement.* The Council will be responsible for:

1. Gathering information and ideas from all faculty through the Liaison Communication Groups.
2. Establishing priorities for schoolwide improvements and organizing special task-force groups.
3. Making decisions on recommendations from task-force groups.
4. Collecting and evaluating evidence of schoolwide improvements.

*Term of Service for Executive Council Members.* The Executive Council will consist of 11 members (9 professionals, 1 administrator, and 1 classified employee). The term of service will begin in January of each school year. Members will serve for three years on a rotating basis. The only exception will be the administrator, who will serve as a member without a rotation.

*Liaison Groups for Communication.* Liaison Groups will meet periodically with their Executive Council representatives to give concerns, ideas, and proposals for schoolwide improvements and to study the effects of schoolwide actions.

*Special Task Forces.* Based on schoolwide concerns for school improvement, special task-force committees will be formed. Each task force will be responsible for making progress reports and recommendations to the Council.

### Decision-Making Procedure of the Executive Council

The following is a summary of the flowchart of the decision-making process of the Executive Council:

Task Force submits recommendations to the Executive Council. Once the Council has sufficient information from the Task Force, the Council will review, revise, accept, or reject the recommendation by consensus. If the Council does not have a consensus on a decision, they will meet within a week (five working days) to try to reach consensus. If consensus at the second meeting is still not forthcoming, a 7–4 majority of the Council will suffice for a final decision.

If the Executive Council feels that a vote is necessary on an issue, then the staff will be afforded the opportunity to vote. When a vote is taken, 80 percent agreement is necessary.

## ITEM 2

### Activities That Compose Each Phase

1. Selecting an area or focus
   - Identify an area of interest
   - Focus on students
   - Look at both immediate and cumulative effects

2. Collecting data
   - Collect existing archival data immediately, then move to conventional and inventive data sources
   - Use multiple data sources
   - Collect data regularly
   - Seek technical assistance if needed (or if things slow down)
   - Promote collective ownership of data
   - Monitor data collection until it becomes normative

3. Organizing data
   - Count instances, events, and artifacts
   - Display data in simple tables and charts
   - Arrange data by classroom, grade level, and school
   - Organize for staff analysis immediately
   - Seek technical assistance, if needed

4. Analyzing and interpreting data
   - Squeeze the data for maximum information
   - Analyze and question the data as a professional collective
   - Determine priority area(s) for action
   - Decide what can be celebrated

Prior to 5: Studying the professional literature
   - Identify topics in the professional literature that relate to or match the school's area of interest
   - Gather research reports, research syntheses, articles, videotapes, etc.
   - Organize these materials for study
   - Analyze and interpret the information in these materials as aids to understanding and to action
   - Determine the most promising actions

5. Taking action
   - Combine information from data analysis with information from professional literature
   - Select "best" options for action
   - Craft short- and long-term action plans
   - Implement some actions immediately
   - Assess implementation of selected actions

1–5. Again and again
   - Use action research to assess effects
   - Use action research to select "new" actions

## ITEM 3a

### Sample Data-Collection Form (Learner)
### Individual Student Log

Beginning Date _____
Ending Date _____

**JUST READ**

Teacher _____ School _____ Grade____
Collection Period _____ to _____

| TITLE OF BOOK | No. of Pages | No. of Minutes | Book Completed YES   NO |
|---|---|---|---|
| 1. | | | |
| 2. | | | |
| 3. | | | |
| 4. | | | |
| 5. | | | |
| 6. | | | |
| 7. | | | |
| 8. | | | |
| 9. | | | |
| 10. | | | |
| TOTALS | | | |

## ITEM 3b

### Sample Data-Collection Form (Learner)
### Classroom Log

| JUST READ | | | | |
|---|---|---|---|---|
| Teacher _____ School _____ Grade____ Collection Period _____ to _____ | | | | |
| Name of Student | No. of Books | No. of Min. | No. of Pages | No. of Compositions |
| | | | | |
| | | | | |
| | | | | |
| | | | | |
| | | | | |
| | | | | |
| | | | | |
| | | | | |
| | | | | |
| | | | | |
| | | | | |
| | | | | |
| Total | | | | |
| Range | | | | |
| Mean | | | | |

**ITEM 4**

**Sample Data Collection Form
(Learning Environment)
Response Form for Implementing a
New Instructional Strategy**

Date _____

Name _____

School _____

Please help us get a picture of your use of the *classification* version of the *inductive model* of teaching during the last week.

How many times did you use it? _____

Please describe the content and objective of one of the uses and materials used. Append a data set, if feasible.

Is there some aspect of the model you'd like help with?

_____

If so, please discuss that aspect briefly.

What do the kids do best with respect to the model?

What do they need the most help with?

## ITEM 5

### Matrix for Processing Books and Articles

### Instructions

Look at each cell in the matrix on the sheet that follows and identify what _____ [author's name] _____ has to offer in regard to the improvement of schooling. Write this information down on the matrix and be prepared to discuss and support your information. **(Note: Enlarge the matrix as it appears in this book.)**

### Key Questions

As an aid to help you scan for this information, the key questions defining each cell are as follows.

#### *Curriculum*

1. What content (knowledge, skill, attitudes) should *students* be experiencing?

2. What content (knowledge, skills, attitudes) should *teachers* be experiencing through activities offered or sponsored by the organization? These activities could be provided by the individual school or the school district.

3. What content (knowledge, skill, attitudes) should *administrators* and *supervisors* be experiencing through activities offered or sponsored by the organization?

#### *Instruction*

4. How should *students* experience the content identified in cell 1? What should classroom instruction look like? How should it be designed, implemented, and evaluated?

5. How should *teachers* experience the content identified in cell 2? What should staff development instruction look like? How should it be designed, implemented, and evaluated?

6. How should *administrators* and *supervisors* experience the content identified in cell 3? What should staff development instruction for administrators and supervisors look like? How should it be designed, implemented, and evaluated?

---

*Note:* In 1987, I developed this generic structured response sheet for use with Goodlad's (1984) *A Place Called School.* Since then, I have used it with many groups to facilitate information processing of complex reports, books, and articles.

### Administration

7. How should the classroom environment be managed for optimum *student* growth? (or) How should the classroom be managed for optimum human resource development of students?

8. How should the classroom environment be managed for optimum *teacher* growth? (or) How should the classroom be managed for optimum human resource development of teachers?

9. How should school systems be managed for optimum *administrator* and *supervisor* growth? (or) How should the school system be managed for optimum human resource development of administrators and supervisors?

### Other

Respond to other prominent concerns in the same way. For example, in a cell called *Assessment*, ask how students, teachers, and administrators and supervisors should be assessed or evaluated—and who would do the assessing.

## Matrix: Processing Books and Articles

| Area of School Improvement | Students | Teachers | Administrators/ Supervisors |
|---|---|---|---|
| Curriculum (What should content be? What knowledge/skills are of most worth?) | 1 | 2 | 3 |
| Instruction (How should the content be presented? What instructional strategies should be used?) | 4 | 5 | 6 |
| Administration (How should the environment be managed?) | 7 | 8 | 9 |

## Item 6

### Responding to Some Common Questions

I respond briefly here to six questions, though I am not sure if there are any perfect responses to them. What I share is more in the nature of reflections than "answers." The topics include reflections on people who are less than eager to participate in collective action—the "resisters." Other questions concern the roles of parents, students, teachers, administrators, and others, as well as the benefits of publishing action plans and reading the professional literature.

### 1. What do we do about resisters?

We ask them to participate in making decisions. We ask them to join us in the actions that the majority deem, through disciplined inquiry and collective reflection, will lead to improvements in student learning and attitudes toward learning. We ask them to suspend prior disbelief in an innovation or change. We ask them to try this innovation or change with us, study its effects on their students, then make the decision to accept it as part of their professional practice or reject it, based on how it affects students.

It is a sad commentary on the social system of many of our schools that so few individuals can block school improvement. Yet the wonderful thing about schools as organizations is that there are few real resisters. Skeptics are not the same as resisters. Skeptics can help us fine-tune our ideas and actions. Resisters seek to block action and deny access. They often simply want things to stay the way they are, even though there are things they do not like—or they simply want to be left alone. When you are leading a major change effort—whether you are a teacher, administrator, or consultant—you often magnify the number of resisters. Sometimes just reflecting on the sparsity of resisters and the abundance of dedicated people seeking to make things better can give you a new perspective.

What we cannot permit in a self-renewing school is for a few members of the organization to block the development of the whole community or to deny students access to greater opportunities for learning. We listen with respect to all members of the organization, and we respond with information or questions. We use their input as part of our reflective inquiry. Although we might wish that our words or political skills would convince others to be advocates, what is of more value would be for them to join us in this cooperative inquiry called schoolwide action research.

In *The Quality School*, Glasser (1990) describes the kind of learning place a school can be. For example, when entering kindergarten, children should discover that each class is a working, problem-solving unit and that each student has both individual and group responsibilities. This is easily translated to describe the kind of workplace a school can be: When staff members join our school, they should discover that it is a problem-solving unit and that each member of the organization has both individual and group responsibilities. Many of our schools would be healthier organizations for us as professionals if they worked more like good kindergarten classrooms.

### 2. Do we really need written action plans, publicly reviewed by the faculty?

Good action plans are like the best curriculum documents: They indicate where the faculty is going, and they provide appropriate guidance for all members of the organization. They publish our disciplined, collective inquiry by describing what we are doing as a professional community and how we will share the results. Whereas the facilitation team or a task force may accept the responsibility of drafting the plan, all faculty members need an opportunity for input and review.

### 3. Do we have to read those research articles?

The collective study of our research base can be a tough task to get started, but it is part of our professional responsibility. If we wish to renew our schools, the study of our professional literature and information generated by others can no longer remain an elitist task of certain central office persons or of our colleagues at the university or of consultants to the district. We all need to become more informed about what works and what does not seem to work and why. To avoid this study and its attendant knowledge and then make decisions that affect whole school populations verges on unethical practice.

On a less somber note, our collective study is a public relations tool that can help us build community support for our actions. We know why we are acting, not because "it" was "mandated" or because it's the year for mathematics curriculum adoption or because the leadership team thinks "it" is a good idea, but because professionals studied the options and made decisions accordingly.

### 4. What do we tell parents? How do we involve parents?

We tell them what we are doing and why: We are professionals studying our craft and working together to improve the education offered our students. We publicize the action research process through our newsletters, parent/teacher meetings, and informal gatherings. When we identify innovations or changes for implementation, we inform parents about these actions and about why we think they will improve student learning or attitudes toward learning. We invite parents' questions, and we ask them to join with us in the initiative.

When a school faculty is just learning the action research process, they may seek less parent involvement than later on when faculty members feel more comfortable with the process. At first, parent involvement often includes participation in surveys or town meetings during which we solicit input through questionnaires and interviews about how much students are using particular skills at home (e.g., How much are they reading, writing, using math, or using social studies?). When faculties are more experienced with cooperative inquiry, they may engage parents more fully in the inquiry (asking them to assist with interviews, assist with the organization and presentation of data, make suggestions about managerial/ administrative problems, participate in implementing the innovations, and engage in goal-setting and problem-solving sessions with the faculty).

Eventually, parents and other community members must become part of the action research process, less for reasons of politics than for reasons of increasing synergy and expanding content.

### 5. What is the role of students in schoolwide action research?

Whenever appropriate, inform students about the schoolwide focus or goal, innovations, and results. We want them to be far more than sources of information in our schoolwide action research. We want them to be constantly involved in their own self-assessment of progress and in the assessment of progress being made by the total learning community.

For example, if an elementary school faculty decided to focus on improved reading comprehension and attitude toward reading, all students could be informed during an assembly and a special kick-off campaign in the classrooms. Students would keep individual logs of the books they have read. In their portfolios, they might keep pictures, descriptions of characters, and short stories predicting what will occur next. Teachers would keep classroom logs of numbers of books read, organized in simple frequency distributions. The facilitation team would keep school logs of number of books read.

Assessments of such a reading campaign would include analyses of videotapes of students reading across the year and analyzing the plot, explaining the actions of characters, and explaining why the setting was especially important to the story. Other assessments could include evaluations of written pieces from the students' portfolios. Students would be involved in their own self-assessment of the number and types of books they are reading, looking at their own logs, writing samples, and videotapes across the year. The teacher might publish weekly the total number of books read; the facilitation team would provide weekly reports organized by grade level, by gender, and any other variable they wish to investigate, in grouped frequency distributions.

In this campaign, one basic question for the faculty is to discover how many students are not reading and to focus sharply on bringing those students to the world of literature (of note, our nonreaders are not always those students with poor learning histories).

We could describe other versions of the preceding scene—using basic math facts, skill in writing, or problem-solving strategies as the focus. At the middle school and high school levels, schoolwide efforts could include campaigns to improve student grades at all levels, increase time present for instruction by reducing tardies and suspensions, or increase global literacy. We could involve the students in collecting and organizing data and reporting the results (even 2nd graders can conduct simple interviews).

Whenever possible, bring students into the inquiry. They are members of our learning community; they are not our subjects. From kindergarten to special education to 12th grade, inform and involve students in attaining the collective goal. We need their assistance to improve student learning.

### 6. What is the role of the teacher? of the principal? of central office staff? of state department of education staff?

People often ask me questions about the role of the principal or central office staff in supporting action research. Occasionally, people ask about the role of state department staff. Only rarely do people ask about the role of the teacher. However, I will address one aspect of the role of the teacher before I consider the other roles.

***Role of the Teacher.*** The teacher is a member of the organization we call the school, but is not alone in educating the youth of the surrounding community. Buildings, resources, colleagueship, and other forms of organizational support are provided. *This recognition of organizational membership is vital to school renewal efforts.* In the self-renewing school, each faculty member accepts responsibility as a professional educator for the success of students who attend his classes; each teacher accepts responsibility as a member of the total learning community, represented formally by the school as an organizational unit, for success in attaining common goals.

***Role of the Principal.*** The principal makes schoolwide action research possible. The principal usually is the primary gatekeeper of what is allowed in as a schoolwide effort. As a formal leader, the principal invites and supports shared governance and collective action over designated areas or over all areas of the school program. Alone, the principal cannot make action research a successful experience; but without the principal as organizational and managerial facilitator, teachers find it almost impossible to successfully pursue schoolwide inquiry. By virtue of organizational position and broader access to information, the principal serves as a full member or an ex-officio member of the facilitation team. But the role of the principal extends far beyond her tasks on the team. The principal participates in schoolwide action research by:

• helping establish the six tangible conditions and three intangible conditions listed in Chapter 3;

- keeping student learning up front;
- using her managerial skills to support the collection, organization, interpretation, and sharing of on-site data and of resources from beyond the school site;
- ensuring appropriate access to information for all faculty members;
- providing continual support and serving as a sounding board for the facilitation team;
- engaging in confrontation when it is necessary for the health of the learning community;
- ensuring that quality staff development is provided to support the implementation of the selected actions; and
- serving as spokesperson for the process with parents, board members, and other community members.

As we study our schools and listen to Fullan and Miles (1992), Huberman (1992), Huberman and Miles (1986), and Miles (1992), we know the value of cross-role leadership, the necessity of arranging time for collaborative/collective work, the need for routines to ensure regular discussion and problem-solving meetings, and the need for technical assistance. Principals secure these necessities.

**Role of Central Office Staff.** Central office staff members encourage and model shared decision making and action research within the district. They support faculties in their efforts, provide technical assistance or locate people who can provide it, provide resources, provide staff development or access to it, help solve problems in relation to time or task demands, provide assistance with group processing if requested, and help tend the health and development of the facilitation team. They help school board members identify and think through policy changes that are needed to support school-based renewal. They also serve as spokespeople for the process with school board members and other members of the community.

**Role of State Department of Education Staff.** State-level staff work to ensure that shared decision making and schoolwide action research are legitimate avenues to school improvement and are supported through state policies. They provide technical assistance or funding for assistance; they provide resources from the professional literature and from other schools or districts engaging in data-driven school renewal; and they help teams from different schools around the state get together for sharing and collaborative problem solving.

**Across the Roles.** All of us are learners, seeking ways to make things better. As this happens, the hierarchy begins to dissolve and become more of a circle of scholars. Behaviors attached to specific roles merge, and we are all responsible for making things work. Our individual changes help create the desirable organizational changes we seek through schoolwide action research.